Life and Culture in NORTHEAST INDIA

For

Vallika** and **Veeha,

Who will take the story forward to
ever-expanding horizons…

Life and Culture in NORTHEAST INDIA

DIPTI BHALLA VERMA AND
SHIV KUNAL VERMA

ABBEVILLE PRESS PUBLISHERS
NEW YORK LONDON

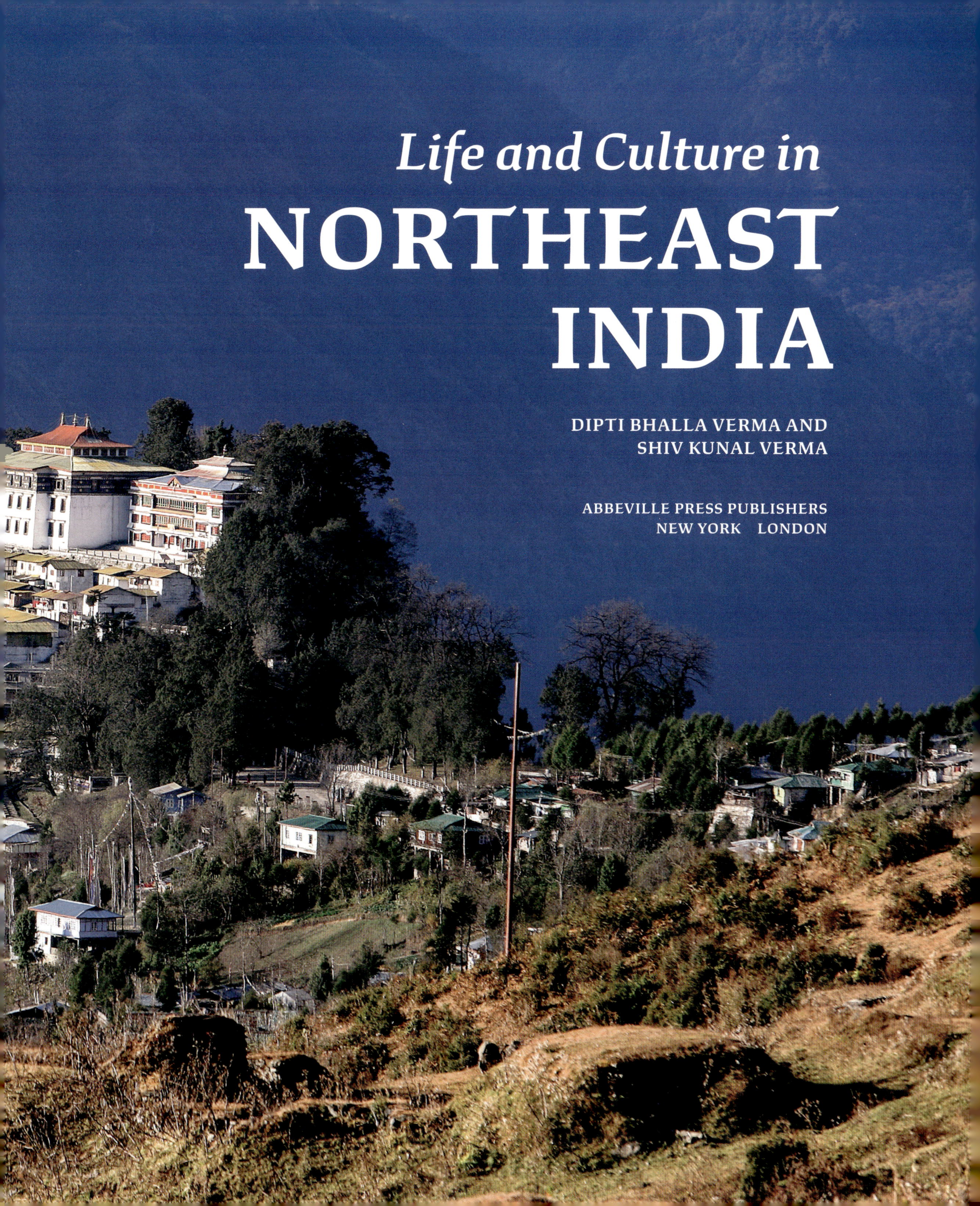

Copyediting: Mithila Rangarajan / Mapin Editorial
Design: Darshit Mori and Gopal Limbad / Mapin Design Studio
Production: Mapin Design Studio

First published in India in 2020 by Mapin Publishing Pvt. Ltd, 706 Kaivanna, Panchvati, Ellisbridge, Ahmedabad 380006 India

First published in the United States of America in 2020 by Abbeville Press, 655 Third Avenue, New York, NY 10017

The text of this book was set in Seravek ExtraLight. Printed in South Korea..

First edition
10 9 8 7 6 5 4 3 2 1

ISBN 978-0-7892-1374-7

Library of Congress Cataloging-in-Publication Data available upon request

For bulk and premium sales and for text adoption procedures, write to Customer Service Manager, Abbeville Press, 655 Third Avenue, New York, NY 10017, or call 1-800-ARTBOOK.

Visit Abbeville Press online at www.abbeville.com.

Captions

PAGE 1 | The Tangkhul are simple people and the women have much the same status as men. Today the prime focus of the Tangkhul is to revive and re-establish their traditional art and culture. Accordingly, certain earlier festivals are still observed. Among these, the eleven-day-long Luira is the most important. It is celebrated with sacrificial offerings and preparation of *khor*, the traditional rice beer.

PAGES 2–3 | Until 1852 the Kanchenjunga Himal was considered to be the highest mountain in the world, with the Singalila Ridge separating Nepal from Sikkim. Calculations made from multiple readings during the Great Trigonometrical Survey of India in 1849 then gave Everest that honour, with Kanchenjunga now being recognised as the third-highest mountain in the world, after K2.

PAGES 4–5 | A Cheetah helicopter's rotors push its limits, rising to these rarefied heights to capture a spectacular view of the less familiar north face of Kanchenjunga. A rare day, when against cloudless skies the planet's third-highest peak paints a magnificent picture.

PAGES 6–7 | The crowning glory of all Khasi festivals is the ancient and hugely popular Ka Pomblang Nongkrem. A thanksgiving ceremony for a good harvest, the celebrations around Nongkrem extend over five days, and the religious rituals often give over to the dancing. It is celebrated every year at Smit village, 11 km (7 mi.) from Shillong. Photograph by Somu John Ingty.

PAGES 8–9 | The Chang, of the central section of the hilly Tuensang District, are believed to have originated from a place known as Changsangmongko. Initially, they settled at Changsang, where *chongnu*, the mythical banyan, grew, giving the tribe its name. The Chang believe that they belong to the same ethno-cultural stock as their neighbours—the Konyak, the Ao, the Khiamngan and the Yimchunger.

PAGES 10–11 | From time immemorial in the Khasi and Jaintia Hills, unspoilt virgin forest, called Law Lyngdoh, has been revered as a sacred grove. Not far from Shillong, the village of Mawphlang has such a forest near it, which has been left undisturbed, as the people believe that the sylvan deities will be offended if the trees are cut or the flowers and fruits plucked.

PAGES 12–13 | Merak Lama Lodre Gyatso founded the Tawang Monastery, whose Tibetan name means "celestial paradise on a clear night". The name "Tawang" itself came from *ta*, Tibetan for "horse", and *wang*, meaning "blessing". Built on a spur, it commands a view of the Gudpi and Chong-Chugmi Ranges, while the valley of the Tawang Chu lies below.

PAGE 16 | During British times the Nyishi were referred to as "Dafla". They sometimes raided the plains of Assam, which in turn lead to military expeditions into the area to "punish the tribes". Contrary to the popular belief that the word *dafla* was used to denote a "savage", it probably originated with the Assamese, who used it to describe a robust physique. For example, a good-looking Assamese girl is even today called a *dafli*.

PAGE 19 | A fusion of styles comes together in this gem-studded, multi-armed Buddha, belonging to the Tripura royal family. The plains of Tripura were under the control of several dynasties that ruled in Eastern Bengal and Samatata during the ancient period. Some of these were of the Buddhist faith, while others were Hindu.

This map has been created based on Record/Master Copy certified by Survey of India. • The responsibility for the correctness of internal details rests with the publisher. • The territorial waters of India extend into the sea to a distance of twelve nautical miles measured from the appropriate base line. • The interstate boundaries amongst Arunachal Pradesh, Assam and Meghalaya shown on this map are as interpreted from the "North-Eastern Areas (Reorganisation) Act. 1971," but have yet to be verified. • The spelling of names in this map have been taken from various sources.

Contents

Foreword

It was almost twenty years ago that Dipti and Kunal made a short film on Manas Wildlife Sanctuary. It was very important as we were all working on the revival of this UNESCO World Heritage Site that had been ravaged due to militancy over the past couple of decades. That was the introduction, but since then we kept in touch because of our common involvement with India's Northeast. Being from the region, I have been a part of some of the journeys with Kunal. It is his images that interpret both the history and the present story of the region, further enhanced by Dipti, who binds them with the right words. Few people in this world realise that a very important part of India begins from here.

How many of us know that the Lepcha have a story akin to Noah's Ark? The entire region described in this book probably has more cultures than the rest of the country put together, and several of the tribal communities place their faith in "biodivinity". Please do not call it "animism", as it is more advanced than the organised religions of the world. Here, they have learnt to depend on their immediate biodiversity for their basic needs of food, clothing and shelter. This is the science of sustainability that our Northeastern communities have been practising for generations, while the world is struggling to achieve sustainable development goals, now that resources have come under tremendous pressure.

Look at the emergence of modern civilisations that were connected through trade: the maritime route, also known as the "rice route", that ran from Chittagong, and the mountain route through Sikkim, known as the "silk route", that connected Lhasa with the rest of the world through this region. These trade routes then introduced the world to a variety of weaving methods, items like terracotta, and agricultural produce that included certain varieties of rice, corn, sweet orange, mango and other produce that are now part and parcel of our daily lives. Every 20 km (12 mi.) that you travel in this region, you will be introduced to a new culture, language and lifestyle, very different in origin, finding their roots somewhere in Asia. A lot of this cultural diversity is also because of the diverse landscape so typical of the Northeast.

Unlike the other great river valleys of India, the Brahmaputra River Valley is still relatively less known. As described in this book, it was not known for a long time that the entry of the Yarlung Tsangpo as the Siang, having negotiated the great bend around the Namcha Barua massif, was in fact the mighty Brahmaputra itself, coming into its own where the waters of the Lohit and Dibang Rivers meet at Sadiya. The Lohit, described by *pandit*s as extending from Brahmagiri to Brahmakund, flows through a landscape where so much has happened along its banks that it will probably need a few hundred books to be described. The spirituality that we boast of today in India is a journey that also encompassed Pragjyotishpur, the area being dominated by the Kamakhya, Hajo and Madan Kamdev Temples, as well as several lost temples. Unlike the rest of the country, the dominance of the matriarchal society still remains the pride of India's Northeast, and much of it is reflected in the weaves and culture of this region.

Even though this book delves into each and every corner of the Northeast as per the current political borders of the states, it focuses on the four major zones with equal intensity, transcending conventional borders. The first of these is the major Kanchenjunga landmark that then extends eastwards as the Assam Himalaya; the second zone comprises the great Brahmaputra and Barak River Valleys and their headwaters; the third is the Jaintia, Khasi and Garo Hills that geographically separate the region from the flood plains of Bangladesh to the south and west; and the very fascinating fourth part is the region that encompasses the Dihing Patkai landscape, extending into Myanmar further to the east, which in recent history was a part of the China-Burma-India theatre during World War II. The pictures and descriptions make this a dream journey through a hitherto under-explored region. This book opens a window that will help you sink into the inner depths of India's Northeast, through the insight of every image and the narrative that is presented through the eyes of Dipti and Kunal.

Raj Basu 大罗

Association for Conservation & Tourism (ACT) is a grass-root level 'not for profit' organization, established in 2001, which has shown the way for Rural Tourism as a tool for empowerment of local communities, helping in poverty alleviation and establishing peace in India's West Bengal & Northeast, Eastern Nepal, Northern Bangladesh, Bhutan and Myanmar.

Introduction

Let there be bliss of good harvest,
Let the earth be full of minerals,
Let the nest of birds be full with eggs and chicks,
Let the earth be filled with wealth,
Let knowledge increase.
The hearth may keep on burning,
So that new leaves may unfold,
So that bamboo may grow and spread,
So that rivers may be full with fish and shrimp,
So that the field is full of grain.
So Mother Mopin,
Let the human cycle of life
Be filled with plenitude.

— Adi Minyong prayer

India's Northeast is a land where nature, in its multifarious physiological and climatic manifestations, has from time immemorial held the lives of the people in the palm of its hands. On the subcontinent, the gap between the Himalayas and the Indian Ocean is at its narrowest here. This geographical factor has resulted in the greatest diversity of insect, plant and animal life. Not so surprising, then, is perhaps the fact that the area also has the largest diversity in the number of human races that have migrated into and made the region their home. The topography of the region may have influenced the migratory patterns over time, but by the beginning of the nineteenth century, this complex web of people had more or less settled down. Survival, then, perhaps depended on each group zealously guarding its ethnicity, a fact that suited the earlier policy of the colonial masters, who furthered the divide in their quest to rule. Like elsewhere in many parts of India, this constant past remains—a reminder of a bygone era, yet coexisting with absolute ease with the evolving present.

The eastern sweep of the Assam Himalayas dominates this incredible landscape, physically defining the northern borders

Step-cultivation is to be widely seen across the mostly hilly terrain of the Northeast wherever there is a village or hamlet. The carefully tended beds offer a picturesque sight, drenched in green.

of the region. The Tsang Po descends into India through a gap in the Great Himalayas at Gelling, flowing through the heart of Adi country as the Siang River, and then debouches into the Assam Plains at Pasighat. There the formidable waters of the Siang mix with the Dibang and the other great tributary, the Lohit, which enters Arunachal Pradesh from Tibet at its extreme northeastern corner at Kibithu. It is here, at the confluence, that the Brahmaputra is born and together the waters flow in a southwesterly direction, annually claiming the plains as their own, swelling and receding across the vast low-lying region of Assam.

Starting from the eastern flank of Arunachal Pradesh, where the warmth of the first rays of the sun are felt, another great north-south mountain chain, the Naga Patkai Hills, extends into Nagaland and Manipur, linking up with the Chaifil Tlang and the Uiphum Tlang Ranges in Mizoram before tapering off into the Chin and the Arakan Yoma. Along the southern bank of the Brahmaputra River are the east-west aligned Jaintia, Khasi and Garo Hills that make up the state of Meghalaya, which in turn separate the river valley from the low-lying areas of Bangladesh to the immediate south. After India's independence and the partition of the subcontinent, the resultant narrow tract of land, the Siliguri Corridor, or "Chicken's Neck", became a slender thread that acted as the sole gateway to the entire region, further extenuating its remoteness and defining its isolation. Once this narrow gap is traversed and the traveller journeys through Sikkim, part of northern West Bengal, Assam, Meghalaya, Arunachal Pradesh, Nagaland, Manipur, Tripura and Mizoram, this often unfamiliar part of the country steps forward in all its geophysical, anthropological and folkloric splendour.

The Himalayan Range is the youngest mountain chain in the world. Ecologically, the region is extremely fragile, prone to landslides and other disturbances. The Assam earthquake of 1950 had virtually altered the face of the Dibang River Valley as entire villages were wiped out. Draining the valleys is a complex network of rivers, all of them tributaries of the Brahmaputra but major rivers in their own right. Often people on either bank have very little to do with each other. Not just the rest of the country but even within the Northeast, communities know very little about each other, most areas having evolved as compartmentalised geographical entities. Until as recently as the early twentieth century, the link between the Tsang Po and the Brahmaputra had yet to be established, with the remoteness of the region it flowed through only adding to its overall mystique.

LEFT | A warrior from the Adi Bobum Bokang tribe guards his village next to the Siang River near Tuting. Until the beginning of the twentieth century, the area was virtually closed to the British owing to violent opposition from the Abor tribes. However, ingress into the region was inevitable if the ground had to be prepared for the drawing up of the international border with Tibet. Due to the increased Chinese influence over the region, Anglo-Chinese relations were strained from the beginning of the previous century.

FACING PAGE
The Adi Shimong are said to have migrated from Tibet to the Nigong Valley. Besides the Adi Ashing that inhabit the area around Tuting, the Adi Tangam migrated to Kuging from the upper gorge of the Siang. The Padam and Pangin tribes downstream stopped their migration further south. Also scattered on the east bank of the Siang are some Idu Mishmi settlements. Though adept at making cane bridges across even the most daunting of rivers, the Adi are generally wary of stepping into rafts or boats to cross the great waters.

This seclusion, however, was and is relative—the Northeast is perhaps the hub through which the country's connectivity with the rest of Southeast Asia can and will develop. The security of the region, both emotionally and tactically, is also vital to India's long-term economic advantage. In the plains and in the hills, many ethnic and sub-ethnic identities exist. Together they share through language, culture, migration and history, as also religion and faith, an anthropological connectivity. Yet this ethnic identity can be a double-edged weapon; it can bring people together or divide them from one another.

India's Northeast was regularly breached by the Burmese in their centuries of conflict with both the Manipuri and Ahom kingdoms, but it was during the Japanese invasion of World War II that the region came into sharp focus. The British opened up the area, pushing the boundaries of their colonial empire; influence and economics were the twin pins on which their policies revolved. World War II changed the profile of the area as the Japanese pushed forward towards the plains of Assam. Ever since, political change has been a constant factor in the lives of the people; the division of Bengal at Independence brought with it its own problems, which contributed to the continued isolation of the region. After Independence the country adopted its own Tribal Policy with respect to the hill areas of the Northeast. This hoped to preserve the existing cultures while at the same time offering the people a collective identity, a participative democratic political system and, essentially, the platform of nationalism to set aside their differences and build towards the future. Nagaland was given its own identity in 1963, Meghalaya in 1972, Mizoram in 1986, and Arunachal Pradesh a year later, in 1987.

FOLLOWING PAGES
Rupa Monastery: The two western districts of Arunachal Pradesh—Tawang and West Kameng—are almost entirely Buddhist. In the Kameng region, the Sherdukpen are concentrated in the Dirang and Singte Valleys and also the Kalaktang (Bomdila) area, while the Monpa are settled in the Tawang Valley.

The Northeast shares international boundaries with Nepal, Bhutan, China, Myanmar (erstwhile Burma) and Bangladesh. This quite naturally has major security implications for the rest of the subcontinent. Further complicating the issue, the general impression of the Northeast today is synonymous with insurgency and underdevelopment, especially in Nagaland and Manipur. Add to this natural disasters, uncontrolled migration, and the displacement of entire peoples—all of which have had a cumulative impact in adding to the constant ferment in which the Northeast finds itself.

In the seven decades that have elapsed since Independence, India as a whole is a changed country as more and more people move across the subcontinent, breaking out of regional and clannish cliques in search of a larger national identity. At the same time, ethnicity, which had always been central to their existence, is now becoming even more critical as they try to cling to their unique lifestyles. Surveys based on linguistic and anthropological data estimate that there are 475 ethnic groups in this region that speak some 400 languages. This mass of some 46 million people therefore offers us a great opportunity to look at one of the most exciting regions of the world, a region of which even today very little is known to the outside world.

At the time of Independence, Arunachal Pradesh—then known as the North-East Frontier Tract (NEFT)—was largely unexplored and, to a great extent, un-administered territory. The British government had been quite content to exercise loose control over the area south of the Great Himalayan wall, secure in the belief that there was no external threat to the Raj from this axis. A handful of people did make inroads into the area, leaving their imprint on the region, which only just allowed for a peep

A Manipuri bride. The beauty of Manipuri women is legendary and the wedding ceremony brings to the fore all the perfection and purity in their Vaishnava practices. The main wedding ceremony of the Meitei is called *luhongba*. It is customary for the bride to wear the Ras Leela skirt.

RIGHT | Tirap District not only shares a border with Nagaland but also houses two Naga tribes—the Nocte and the Wancho, or the Eastern Nagas—ethnically related to the Konyak tribe. The Nocte inhabit southwestern and central parts of the district and account for forty-five per cent of its tribal population.

FACING PAGE
Heads of cattle dot the Khasi countryside. Meghalaya lies to the south of Assam, the hilly areas between the Brahmaputra Valley to the north and the low riverine plains of Bangladesh to the south. Geographically known as the Meghalaya Plateau or the Shillong Plateau, it is an important part of the Northeast's topography.

into the mist-shrouded valleys of dense jungles and fierce warlike tribes. Notable among them were Colonel Frederick Marshman Bailey and Captain Henry Triese Morshead, who ventured into the Dibang Valley and then surveyed and charted the entire Himalayan watershed. Their work greatly influenced the demarcation of the McMahon Line that was drawn up in 1914 between the British and the Tibetans. (Tracing their initial route up to Yonggyap La, the authors successfully managed to photograph the pass, from where the massif of Namcha Barua was also clearly visible [see page 127]).

Others followed—Frank Kingdon-Ward, the renowned botanist and naturalist, who not only did pioneering work on the flora of Assam but also solved the mystery of the "Great Brahmaputra Falls"; the anthropologist Christoph von Fürer-Haimendorf, who was the first to venture into Apatani and Dafla (Nyishi) areas at the time; Major Ralengnao "Bob" Khathing, who led the Assam Rifles detachment into what was then known as the Towang Salient, in 1951, and established the writ of the Government of India; Verrier Elwin, a confidant of Mahatma Gandhi who, with Prime Minister Jawaharlal Nehru, helped shape India's Tribal Policy, and many more.

Till the 1960s, the North-East Frontier Agency (formerly NEFT) was an evolving entity as independent India grappled with huge problems, not least of which were its newly defined borders. From a strategic point of view, the narrowness of the Chicken's Neck area, the challenge of poor or no road connectivity, and hostile weather conditions through the year magnified the isolation of the Northeast, to say nothing of NEFA and the Naga Patkai hill regions.

Over the seven decades since Independence, India has demonstrated the ability to survive, to knit together one of the most complicated webs of humanity, and in the process also secure the ethnic and cultural identity of the people. However, national identity cannot take a back seat over regional identity, especially as improved forms of communication propel the world

FOLLOWING PAGES
Of the nine districts in Manipur, five are located in the hills. A tribal population inhabits these districts, which are dominated by the Naga and the Kuki, as opposed to the valley which is a stronghold of the Meitei community. Rice farming in the hills is practised through *jhum* cultivation, while in the Imphal Valley, traditional farming methods are in practice.

away from geographical insularity. It then becomes critically important for all of us to understand not just ourselves, but the entire whole. On a larger canvas, the pieces and their interdependence become obvious. It is therefore imperative for us to know what all the pieces look like. Too often in the past, the links between these pieces were forgotten, or set aside deliberately.

Falguni Rajkumar, in his book *Rainbow People*, writes of Mera Haou Chogba, a festival celebrated in Manipur. Every evening, every Meitei household would light a lamp and raise it on a tall bamboo pole in the courtyard of their home. These lights, visible from the hills surrounding the Imphal Valley, were a signal from the younger brother (the Meitei) to the elder brother (the surrounding hill tribes) that they were safe and happy in their homes. With emerging technology, exciting schemes like the Kolodyne River Project form the bedrock of the Look East Policy that hopefully will lead to greater stability in the region.

In the Indian psyche, both Sikkim and North Bengal have been delinked from the Northeast. The remaining states that were carved out of Assam, along with Manipur and Tripura, are referred to as the Seven Sisters. This, however, defies geographical logic, for the Kanchenjunga massif, which has dominated the north-south Singalila Range since Sikkim became a part of India in 1972, marks the western extremity and separates the region from the rest of the subcontinent.

The Eight States of Northeast India

Therefore in today's context, Sikkim, standing at the gateway to the Northeast, is our natural starting point in the book. Nye-

ABOVE | Mizo youth dressed in weaves of red, orange and black and decked out in traditional jewellery revel in song and dance.

CENTRE | Come October, the Garo Hills begin to reverberate to the sound of drumbeats that announce to the world the start of Wangala, the most important festival of the Garo people. Offerings are made to honour Misi Saljong, the god of fertility who presides over crops and controls the rain, water and growth of all things. Music flows from flutes, gongs and buffalo-horns and the village gathers together for seven days and nights of dance, feasting, rice-beer drinking and revelry.

BELOW | The loom goes *clack-clack* and a rich palette of colours emerges as the women weave, revealing time and time again the unerring aesthetic sense of tribal communities.

Mayelyang, or "a hidden heaven on earth", was the name given by the Lepcha, who arrived at the base of "Khangchendzonga" in search of new lands in ancient times. The mountain, the guardian deity of Sikkim, dominates the northwestern part of a predominantly mountainous state. Sikkim shares its northern and northeastern borders with Tibet, and to the west and east are Nepal and Bhutan, respectively, while North Bengal's Darjeeling District connects it to the rest of India. By the fifteenth century the Bhutia, along with Buddhism, arrived from Tibet, followed by the Nepalese and Hinduism a few centuries later. The glacier-laden and wind-swept Sikkim Plateau, from where arises the Teesta River, lakes like the Khecheopalri and the Gurudongmar, the famous Nathu La and Jalep La passes, and a landscape dotted with monasteries—Dubdi, Rumtek, Tsuklakhang, Enchey, Sangachoeling and Tashiding among them—complete the picture of this erstwhile Himalayan kingdom. Recently, in a move that will hopefully help conserve the ecology of the region further, the Khangchendzonga National Park has been declared a World Heritage Site by the United Nations Educational, Scientific and Cultural Organization (UNESCO).

Darjeeling, along with the areas around Siliguri, Jalpaiguri and Cooch Behar, is linked by the Duars that connect us to Assam. This region remains one of the most spectacular in terms of natural beauty. The forests around Alipur Duar, namely, Jaldapara and the Buxa Tiger Reserve, have yielded some of the largest elephant specimens in recorded history.

To this day, the whole of the Northeast is just "Assam" to most people. Sitting at the heart of region, the state from which many of the other states were carved, Assam has international borders with Bhutan and Bangladesh and state borders with West Bengal, Arunachal Pradesh, Nagaland, Manipur, Mizoram, Tripura and

The Hojagiri dance of the Reang is performed with delicate balance and poise. Silver ornaments—particularly the distinctive coin necklace *rangbauh*, which also bestowes a high status—have pride of place in the women's attire. Ethnic clashes and persecution by the Mizo forced the Reang to leave their homes in Mamit and Lunglei Districts. They continue to languish in camps in Tripura that have since claimed several lives.

Meghalaya. Hill tracts surround the low-lying Brahmaputra plains, the river entering the state at the northeastern end and flowing across it before entering Bangladesh at the southwest extreme. Assam, which derives its name from the Sanskrit word *asoma*, meaning "peerless and unparalleled", has woven a rich fabric with its multi-ethnic composite culture, starting with the autochthon Bodo; the Ahom, who swept in from the eastern hills in the twelfth century and ruled for six centuries; the Tai Khampti; and, finally, the advent of British India, bringing in East Bengalis, Biharis and Oriyas. An agricultural state, Assam's tea industry and the endless tea gardens have caught the imagination of the world.

From its western border with Bhutan to its eastern frontier with Myanmar, the Himalayan sweep of Arunachal Pradesh brackets the north for 1,030 km (640 mi.). A further stretch of 441 km (274 mi.), dipping southeastwards along the Naga Patkai Hills, rounds off this state at 83,743 sq km (32,333 mi.). It could well be defined as the eastern Land of Five Rivers, much like Punjab in the west. The five major river systems, namely, Kameng, Subansiri, Dibang, Siang and Lohit, along with their numerous streams and tributaries, complete the picture.

A colourful mix of the modern and the old, the capital city of Aizawl dominates the otherwise sparsely populated landscape of Mizoram.

Historically, religion in Arunachal Pradesh can be seen in three parallel geographical layers—primarily Hinduism in the foothills in Upagiri; animism extending across the central belt, Antagiri; and Buddhism dominating the upper reaches of the Eastern Himalayas, Vahigiri. Today there is much more mobility, geographic and otherwise, seen amongst the different communities. Of the 110 tribes and sub-tribes, the Monpa, Sherdukpen and the Aka reside in the West Kameng District; the Nyishi, Tagin, Apatani and Hill Miri are to be found eastward in the Subansiri region; the Adi, Memba, Khamba and Mishing are astride the Siang; and the Mishmi, Khampti and Singpho are settled in the Lohit District. The Nocte and the Wancho make up the Tirap end.

The story of Nagaland the way the tribes recount it emerges from the ancient mists of time, handed down from generation to generation through oral traditions and from the accounts of those who helped open up this region. Among them, the works of Fürer-Haimendorf, James Philip Mills, Ursula B. Graham and Elwin reveal the multifaceted tribal world, which until recently was shrouded in a veil of inaccessibility. We observe the Angami, Ao, Konyak, Chang, Wokha, Sema, Lotha, Rengma, Chakhesang and many other tribes. Their clashes with the British as the latter tried to make inroads into the region are legendary. Then came Independence and the ensuing unrest that added to the further isolation of the region.

Manipur, which literally translates to "Jewel State", has a proud history with the Vaishnava dynasty of its Meitei community. It has a culturally rich pre-Hindu Sanamahi past, combined with a tradition of art and classical dance drama. While the Manipur Valley is Meitei-dominated, five of its nine districts are located in the hills and peopled by diverse Naga and Kuki tribes.

The Manipuri had taken on the British Raj headlong in 1890, but were eventually subdued by superior military force. The Kuki, in turn, continued to resist the British for the next fifty years, refusing to be subjugated. Post Independence, insurgency in Manipur began in the mid-1950s as an ideological movement for the restoration of the pre-British Meitei supremacy. The movement soon turned into an ethnic conflict, while the simultaneous growth of Naga militancy, with its close links to the Manipur Naga (mainly Tangkhul Naga), made it more of a political power struggle. Historically, the tribes—aligning, re-aligning, grouping and regrouping themselves in order to consolidate their own positions in the complex social hierarchy of the state—have dissipated a lot of energy. As a result, the common citizen often finds himself caught in the crossfire between the multiple underground organisations and security forces even today.

Mizoram literally means "Land of the Highlanders". The first Mizo who settled in India were known as "Kuki" and subsequent immigrants were called "New Kuki". The Mizo are believed to be Mongolian in origin and migrated into India from China. Topographically, the hills rise steeply, varying from 1,000 to 2,210 metres (3,279 to 7,248 ft.) (Phawngpui, or "the Blue Mountain"). Rivers cut deep gorges between the hills and flow either northwards or southwards. There are splendorous lakes with musical names like Palak, Tamdil, Rangdil and Rengdil. There is an attempt to unite all Mizo wherever they live. Tribes of several ethnic groups are linked either culturally or linguistically and form the Lushai/Lusei or Mizo, both umbrella terms bringing two-thirds of the populace together in today's Mizoram. The Chakma, the Lai and the Mara are the other major tribes that mainly inhabit southern Mizoram.

Before descending back into the plains, on the southern flank of the Brahmaputra rise the Jaintia, Khasi and Garo Hills, which, like the Himalayan Range to their north, run east to west. Meghalaya literally means "Abode of Clouds". Geologists believe that this picturesque part of the country was, in fact, once a coral island rising from the sea. The tribes that inhabit the plateau and valleys in these hills trace their origin to pre-Aryan times. The Khasi are Mon-Khmers, sharing a megalithic culture with the Jaintia, while the Garo are Tibeto-Burmese, of the Bodo group. Meghalaya was under the parallel rule of these three dominant tribes till the British gradually annexed it. This is the story of tribal life, where traditional structures like a matrilineal society, which have stood the test of time, coexist with Christianity and the urbanisation that gradually gained a foothold. It was only in 1972 that Meghalaya attained full statehood in the Union of India.

The Barak River Valley dominates southern Assam, which drops down from the Karbi region to Silchar, with the Naga Patkai to the east and the Jaintia Hills to the west. Partly owing to the low-lying terrain and the influence of the Barak waters, the region is a major "food basket", with agriculture being one of the main occupations of the people. Historically, the entire link of southern Assam and the Barak River Valley has been exclusively through East Bengal. The Barak River enters the Karimganj District through its northeastern corner near Badarpurghat, after which it divides itself into two branches at Haritikar—the Surma and the Kushiara.

Finally, we come to the ancient land of Tripura that is tucked into the southwestern corner of the Northeast, bordered by Bangladesh to the west, by Assam to the north and south and then Mizoram to the east. Ruled from the eighth century till Independence by a single Kshatriya dynasty, it is believed to have ancestral links with the "Lunar" dynasty of the *Mahabharata*. Tradition has it that Yayati's son, Druhyu, came eastward and settled in Pragjyotishpura.

During Partition, a large chunk of Tripura, even though it was an independent kingdom, was ceded to East Pakistan (later Bangladesh) and thousands of immigrants flowed into the state that till then had majorly comprised its autochthons—the Dev Barman, Tripuri, Jamatia and the Reang, along with a few others. Thereafter, most of the tribal population was pushed up into the hills, and today the tribal populations form a small fraction of the state's population. The kingdom of Tripura was one of the last princely states to join the Union of India, in 1949.

Sikkim

In a remote corner of India, tucked away in the Eastern Himalayas, a Bungthing invokes his gods. From the time the first settlers came to this hidden land, this is a scene that has often played out in the forest, since the Lepcha worship nature as the ultimate form of creation. Beyond the world's third-highest mountain, Kanchenjunga, at 8,686 m (28,497 ft.), extend the great Assam Himalayas that stretch from Sikkim to Arunachal Pradesh. The Kanchenjunga massif, also known to the rest of the world as "the Mountain of Gold", dominates the Singalila Range and is revered by virtually all people, regardless of which faith they follow. If ever there was a landscape that inspires awe it is certainly this endless and formidable treasure of the Eastern Himalayas. In many ancient Hindu texts it is called Indrakil, or "the Garden of Lord Indra". During the annual Pang Lhabsol festival, the lamas of Pemayangtse Monastery in West Sikkim invoke the blessings of Khangchendzonga, Sikkim's guardian deity, to protect the land and take care of the people.

The rugged and impassable Assam Himalayas throw out two equally enormous spurs—the Singalila Range that separates Sikkim from Nepal to its west and the Chola Range that divides the state from the Chumbi Valley and Bhutan to the east. These

Nathu La, "the Listening Ears Pass", at 4,310 m (14,140 ft.), a traditional part of the Old Silk Route, linked the plains of South Bengal to Lhasa in Tibet, traversing a distance of 563 km (349 mi.). Today manned by defence personnel, with no permanent human habitation and only an array of endangered species of animals for company, it opens for trade and visitors only during the summer months.

two mountain ranges form a gigantic amphitheatre, a maze of tangled interlacing ridges that rise range after range to the icy heights that are the perennial abode of the snows.

The Tibetan Plateau borders the North Sikkim Plateau, which, at an average altitude of 5,182 m (17,000 ft.), is home to some spectacular geographical features. The Kerang Bowl houses a glacier from where the Teesta River originates. Then there is the Gurudongmar Lake, which according to legend never completely freezes over, always leaving a small spot in the middle that is believed to be the blessing of revered saints like Guru Padmasambhava and Guru Nanak. This rain shadow area of the Kanchenjunga, a bleak and barren landscape given to extreme cold and blizzards, is even today the home of the nomadic herdsmen and their flocks of sheep intermingled with the shaggy yaks.

Moving eastward from Gangtok, past the Tsangu Lake, at an altitude of 4,310 m (14,140 ft.) lies Nathu La, one of the three traditional passes that connected Tibet and India. Even on a clear day, it is difficult to breathe here, and added to this is the wind chill factor. The pass was reopened after five decades for bilateral trade in 2006. Indian traders are allowed to set up shop a few kilometres inside China and, similarly, the Chinese can come down to Sherathang. Beyond lies the Chumbi Valley, where the boundaries of India, China and Bhutan meet.

It is believed that in ancient times the Lepcha, who are of Mongolian racial stock, resided in Southeast China. Their search for new lands brought them to the base of the Kanchenjunga. They recognized this to be the land of their quest; Sikkim was their own Nye-Mayelyang, "a hidden heaven on earth", where the sacred rivers Rangit (Re-Nye) and Teesta (Tashi-Drag) flowed through the valleys. The Tibetan name for Sikkim is Denjong, or "Valley of Rice", while the Bhutia call it Beyul Demazon, or "Hidden Valley of Rice".

Da-chos, or prayer flags, breezily paint the landscape of Sikkim, particularly in places of pilgrimage, where they are strung out gaily, carrying luck in every direction as though riding an airy horse.

FACING PAGE
The Gurudongmar Lake, seen here in all its pristine beauty at the height of winter, is bedecked with prayer flags in summer when the snow recedes.

The History of Sikkim

An early historical record of the Lepcha, *Chunakh-Aakhen*, recounts how King Pohartuk Panu sent troops to Takshila to join Chandragupt Maurya's defense against Alexander the Great's invading armies. Sikkim's early phase, predating the eighth century, is highlighted by the visit of Guru Padmasambhava, the Indian saint who is also known as Guru Rinpoche to the Buddhists, while on his way to Tibet. It is believed that the Lepcha kingdom may have extended up to the Sun Kosi River in Nepal at one time. In the fifteenth century, Turve, a man of legendary vision, carved out the political boundaries of what would later become the Kingdom of Sikkim. He unified the Lepcha and Limbu confederations and was conferred the title of Punu, or King, for his achievements.

The ultimate forest dwellers, completely at ease and in harmony with nature, the Lepcha knew the ways of the primal forests and had an inherent and extensive zoological and botanical nomenclature of their own.

ABOVE RIGHT | Among the spectacular lakes of the upper reaches of East Sikkim is the Bithang Chu Lake. Like the other lakes this, too, is glacial in origin, scooped out as a hollow and filled with glacial melt over time. Surrounded by rugged mountains, it seems to mirror the sky with its azure hues.

RIGHT | A Lepcha denizen of Dzongu happily poses for us with his dog. He is dressed in the traditional knee-length *pagi* worn by Lepcha males, woven in striped cotton and secured with a belt. The hairstyle of the Lepcha is a plaited pigtail.

FACING PAGE
ABOVE | The yak is a hardy and reliable helpmate of the Sikkimese people, well able not only to survive but also thrive at high altitudes. The Yak Chaam, a form of religious dance, is a tribute to this enduring friendship between man and beast.

BELOW | The heartland of Sikkim that encompasses the confluence of the Lachen and Lachung Rivers is the home of the Lepcha. The rugged terrain of Dzongu has given the Lepcha the name "Ravine Folk".

UNESCO World Heritage Site

Khangchendzonga National Park

In 1977, the first Wildlife Protected Area in Sikkim was notified and named the Kanchenjunga National Park (KNP). Two decades later, a buffer zone was also demarcated, with an additional 836 sq km (322 sq. mi.) being declared a protected area. Renamed the Khangchendzonga National Park, this biosphere reserve, covering an area of 2,620 sq km (1,011 sq. mi.), was designated a UNESCO World Heritage Site in July 2016.

The park extends northwards from the Yuksom Plateau in West Sikkim and spreads into North Sikkim, taking in its sweep the high altitude area around

The rugged snow-covered sweep of the Kanchenjunga ridge dominates the western landscape and the Nepal Peak. The north is presided over by Tent Peak and the ridge of the Zemu glacier; the east is bound by Mt Lamaongden, while the Narsing and Pandim mountains form the southern boundary.

ABOVE | Brought back from the brink of extinction, the red panda, almost a fantasy creature, is symbolic of this biosphere reserve. Photograph by Dhritiman Mukherjee.

the Kanchenjunga massif. The Yuksom Plateau, in all probability the residue of an ancient hanging glacier, is bounded on three sides by steep gorges, merging on the northeastern side with the steeply rising slopes of the Kanchenjunga. The vegetation consists of the temperate broad-leaved forest that is mostly undisturbed, where the closed canopy of trees covered by mosses and other epiphytes are typical. The dominant trees are *Quercus lamellosa*, *Quercus pachyphylla*, *Magnolia campbellii*, *Machilus edulis*, *Castanopsis hystrix*, *Juglans regia*, *Symplocos theifolia*, *Michelia excelsa*, *Rhododendron griffithianum*, *Cinnamomum obtusifolium* and *Taxus wallichiana*. Most of the forest is covered by dense undergrowth of dwarf bamboo and various species of rhododendrons.

In a highly rugged mountainous terrain like that of Sikkim, where the elevation ranges from about 800 m (2,400 ft.) in the south to about 8000 m (5 mi.) in the northwestern corner, it is very difficult to expect lakes. Nevertheless, the state is endowed with some of the most picturesque lakes of the Himalayan terrain. The entire area has several lakes of various sizes. Most of these originated as hollows, scooped out by the glaciers in the valleys through which they flowed, subsequently filled by glacial melt. Others were formed by the damming of glacial water by terminal moraines. As we gain in altitude, the forest type changes to temperate coniferous alongside the broad-leaved trees. The vegetation is mixed conifer, comprising species such as silver fir (*Abies densa*), hemlock (*Tsuga brunoniana*) and spruce (*Picea smithiana*), interspersed with junipers.

Species such as *Larix griffithiana*, *Taxus wallichiana*, *Acer caudatum*, *Rhododendron arboreum*, *Rhododendron campanulatum*, *Rhododendron grande* and *Betula utilis* are also found. Numerous undergrowth species such as *Berberis*, *Ilex*, *Pyrus*, *Ribes*, *Rubus*, *Spiraea*, *Viburnum* and *Herbaceous arisaema* are common in this zone. These two zones are particularly rich in their avifauna. A systematic study of the birds of Sikkim was first undertaken during the nineteenth century, focusing on taxonomy and systematics. The subsequent study by Dr. Salim Ali is the most comprehensive and exhaustive work on the birds of Sikkim till date. Ali extensively reviewed past studies, substantiating them with field surveys, and published a book containing a detailed list of 524 species distributed in Sikkim. During the last fifteen years, different institutions

Among the wide variety of flowering plants, the rhododendron (*Rhododendron niveum*) adds a luxurious splash of colour. It is the state tree, with an array of 36 species.

FACING PAGE
ABOVE | The red panda (*Ailurus fulgens*) is the much-loved state animal and is seen walking along the pathways and the wide-spreading branches of its arboreal home.

BELOW | The endless rugged terrain is laced with frothing streams and waterfalls that spontaneously appear every rainy season.

and researchers have added another 50 species based on field studies. The avifaunal wealth of Sikkim comprises around forty-five per cent of the total bird species found in the Indian subcontinent. These 574 species of birds are represented under 253 genera, 55 families and 16 orders. *Garrulax* is the richest genus, comprising 15 species. Other rich genera are *Carpodacus* (10 species), *Ficedula* and *Turdus* (9 species each), and *Alcippe* (8 species). Similarly, the family *Sylviidae* represents the maximum number of species (116), followed by *Muscicapidae* (82 species), *Corvidae* (39 species), *Fringiilidae* (32 species), *Accipiteridae* (29 species), and *Passeridae* (28 species).

Heading into the immediate Kanchenjunga region, the subalpine vegetation takes over. Trees and shrubs become stunted and the tree line appears at around 4000 m (2 mi.), where evergreen coniferous forests are replaced by rhododendrons, azaleas, and flowering herb species such as *Potentilla*, *Anemone*, *Primula*, *Ligularia* and *Pedicularis*.

Finally, this brings us to the alpine zone—with an elevation of more than 4500 m (2 mi.), this zone represents the Greater Himalayas and remains under snow cover for almost six to seven months a year. This area is known for its spectacular range of pheasants—*Lophura leucomelanos* and *Gallus gallus* are commonly observed pheasants in low-elevation forests, *Tragopan satyra* occur in mid-elevation, whereas *Lerwa lerwa* and *Tetraogallus tibetanus* are pheasants of high elevations.

Aquatic avifauna are also well represented in Sikkim but most are migratory in nature. Some of the species that occur in the state are *Anser indicus*, *Mergus merganser*, *Anas platyrhynchos*, *Aythya baeri*, *Aythya ferina* and *Tadorna*

Khangchendzonga National Park

ABOVE LEFT | The eternal mist-swathed dawn in Dzongu, and the looming bodyguards of Kanchenjunga.

ABOVE RIGHT | The Sikkim stag, painted here in all its glory, is now extinct.

LEFT | The spotted laughing thrush, a part of Sikkim's avian family, which numbered 574 species of birds at last count. Photograph by Dhritiman Mukherjee.

FACING PAGE
The red-billed leiothrix (*Leiothrix lutea*) in a bamboo clump. Photograph by Dhritiman Mukherjee.

ferruginea. Distinct turnover of species has been observed along vegetation/elevation gradients; the avifaunal assemblage changes rapidly from tropical to subtropical, temperate to alpine, and finally, to cold desert forms. The tropical and subtropical belts, with elevations up to 1800 m (1 mi.), harbour maximum avifaunal diversity in Sikkim.

The high-elevation areas towards the subalpine and alpine zones harbour very unique assemblages of birds. The cold, dry and windy environment of this region is dominated by various species of rosefinches, snowfinches, accentors, larks, buntings, pipits and redstarts. Other species such as *Lerwa lerwa*, *Tetraogallus tibetanus*, *Ithaginis cruentus*, *Columba leconota*, *Syrrhaptes tibetanus*, *Calidris temminckii*, *Pseudopodoces humilis*, *Pyrrhocorax pyrrhocorax*, *Pyrrhocorax graculus* and *Corvus corax* also occur. The threatened black-necked crane species (*Grus nigricollis*) has been reported to occur in the alpine zone in Sikkim.

TOP | The blood pheasant (*Ithaginis cruentus*) is the state bird of Sikkim.

CENTRE | The Impeyan *monal* (*Lophophorus impejanus*) is a proud flag-bearer of the pheasant family.

RIGHT | Numerous glacier-fed rivers and streams wend their way down from the mountains, the Rathang River being one of them.

Photographs by Dhritiman Mukherjee.

As observed in other faunal groups, distinct turnover of mammalian fauna can be noticed along the vegetation/elevation gradient in Sikkim. Assamese macaques and barking deer are common mammals of the tropical forests. Similarly, the red panda, which is the state animal, the common langur, Himalayan black bear, lesser cats, *goral* and *serow* are dominant mammalian fauna of the temperate broad-leaved forests in Sikkim. Mammals such as musk deer, the Himalayan *tahr*, blue sheep and the Himalayan marmot occur in the upper reaches of coniferous and subalpine to alpine meadows.

The Trans-Himalayan region towards the Tibetan plateau is an important region that harbours various threatened species such as *kiang* (*Equus kiang*), *nayan* (*Ovis ammon*), the Tibetan gazelle, snow leopard, and the Tibetan wolf. Most of the species occurring in the Greater Himalayan and Trans-Himalayan zones have small home ranges and aggregate along the northern border of the Tibetan Plateau. Because of dwindling populations and anthropogenic pressure, they remain vulnerable in the range of their habitats in Sikkim.

TOP | The satyr tragopan (*Tragopan satyra*) in a snowfield.

CENTRE | The *bharal* (*Ovis nivicola*), or snow sheep, makes an appearance atop the rocks.

LEFT | The snow leopard (*Panther uncia*) is almost camouflaged by a terrain of shrubs and rocks that complements its own hues.

Photographs by Dhritiman Mukherjee.

Alongside the Lepcha, the Limbu form the other major community considered to be the indigenous people of Sikkim. They migrated into Nepal from Tibet mainly from the southern banks of the Tsang Po River. It is believed that the name "Limbu" was given by the Nepalese, for they called themselves "Yakthumba", which meant "yak-herders". Later, the Lepcha and the Bhutia called them "Tshong", which in the vernacular meant "traders". The Limbu followed a religion called Yumaism, which is deeply influenced by both Lamaism and Hinduism, with shamans being major players in all religious activities.

Legend has it that in the mid-thirteenth century, the Kham king Khye Bhumsa and his wife, who were childless, were advised by the lamas to seek the guidance of Thekung Tek, a reputed Lepcha seer. With a band of followers the king made the journey from Tibet down the Chumbi Valley and sought the Lepcha chief in his forest home. Thekung Tek made a prophecy that the king would have three sons and this proved to be true. Thereafter, a blood brotherhood was sworn between the Bhutia and the Lepcha by which the latter agreed that the Bhutia could settle in Sikkim and that the two tribes would live thenceforth in harmony as friends. To mark this pact, the Lepcha chief erected nine stones facing Kanchenjunga at Kabi Longstok, where they stand till today.

The Bhutia came to be known as Denzongpa, "Denzong" being their name for Sikkim and *pa* meaning "inhabitants". Intermarriage between the two communities increased social and cultural assimilation. Though Khye Bhumsa had returned to the Chumbi Valley, his three sons and their subsequent clans established themselves in the immediate vicinity of Gangtok. They, however, retained their close links with Tibet. The Bhutia practiced the Nyingmapa and Kagyupa Tibetan schools of Buddhism and began converting the Lepcha to their faith. Soon the parity between the two communities became a thing of the past as the migrant community became dominant, especially as Buddhism took hold.

In 1642, when three lamas arrived in Yuksom, Lamaism, a mixture of Buddhism with mythology and mysticism, had

At Kabi Longstok, Khye Bumsa, the Bhutia king, and the Lepcha chief Thekung Tek swore a blood brotherhood. To mark this momentous occasion the Lepcha chief erected nine stones facing Kanchenjunga, where they still stand today.

LEFT | For the Limbu, Yuma, Kapoba and Theba tribes, household gods are propitiated for general well-being and invoked in times of trouble for the family. This totem is part of the ritual to expel evil.

It was here at Yuksom in West Sikkim where the three lamas assembled in 1642 to decide on a temporal and spiritual head. Thereafter, Phuntsong Namgyal was crowned the first *chogyal*, or king, of Sikkim, heading the Namgyal dynasty.

TOP | The faith healer, known as the *jhankri*, must first determine which spirit is causing harm to the family, after which they either placate the spirit, or drive it away by having family members feverishly sound pots and pans and/or hit it vigorously with a broom.

become the most powerful hierarchy in Tibet. The doctrine of incarnate lamas and the worship of the enlightened saints had become prominent features in the faith. Buddhism and Lamaism, having originated in India prior to flourishing in Tibet, were back in India. The wheel had turned a full circle.

The crowning of Khye Bhumsa's grandson, Phuntsong Namgyal, as the king of Sikkim completed the ascendancy of the Bhutia. Folklore says that the three lamas converged at Yuksom from three different directions and agreed that Sikkim needed a spiritual and temporal head to further propagate Buddhism. Thus, Phuntsong Namgyal was summoned from Gangtok and consecrated by the priests as the first *chogyal*, or king, of Sikkim. The *chogyal*s were to rule until the end of the institution in 1975.

As the Lepcha readily accepted the external expressions of Buddhism, the first *gompa*s and monasteries rose to preserve the memory of the missionary monks. The oldest monastery in Sikkim was Dubdi, built by the newly ordained *chogyal* in

honour of the most senior lama, Lhatsun Chhembo. The other two lamas were honoured with more modest shrines—Kathok and Wodsalling. Sangachoeling Monastery was established and declared open to all—the Lepcha, the Limbu and the Bhutia.

The *chogyal* now needed to bring all the major communities under his direct power. A convention of the tribal leaders was called, where Phuntsong Namgyal announced that they were of one family and would form a governing council called Lho-Men-Tsong-Sum. The treaty was signed by twenty-four men, eight of whom were Bhutia ministers, twelve of whom were Limbu and four Lepcha. With the treaty of Lho-Men-Tsong-Sum and the defining of the state's borders, Sikkim was firmly established as a kingdom.

In 1670 CE, Tensung Namgyal ascended the throne and moved his capital to Rabdentse. The *chogyal* married three times. His first wife was from Bhutan, the second from Tibet, and the third was from the Limbuwan region. The third wife, Thungwamukma, coined the word *sukhim*, which meant "a new house" in Limbu terminology. This later on became "Sikkim".

The third *chogyal*, Chagdor Namgyal, ascended the throne at the tender age of 14. However, Pendi Wangmo, his half-sister from his Bhutanese stepmother, contested the accession. It wasn't long before the raja of Bhutan jumped into the fray and sent troops to assassinate the young boy, who was quickly whisked away to Tibet by his loyal ministers. For eight years the Bhutanese controlled Rabdentse but were finally asked to withdraw from Sikkim by Tibetan authorities. In 1707 the *chogyal* returned to Rabdentse, where he devoted most of his energies to further promoting Buddhism. In 1717, he was assassinated, and his Bhutanese half-sister was found guilty of abetting the murder and was strangled to death.

During this period, Pemayangtse Monastery emerged as the largest Nyingma monastery and reserved the right to the enrolment of monks from Sikkimese Bhutia families of "pure descent". It is only the monks of this monastery who enjoy the title of Dratsang, "pure monks of the Bhutia race", and they would have the honour of crowning all subsequent *chogyal*s. Tashiding Monastery, from its inception, became one of the main Nyingmapa monasteries in Sikkim and is famous for its most holy *chorten* known as Thong-Wa-Rang-Dol, meaning "saviour by mere sight".

Territorial problems with Bhutan were to continue in the east. But 1774 onwards, there were a series of skirmishes with the Gorkhas in the west, lead by Prithvi Narayan, along the banks of the Arun River, the boundary between Nepal and Sikkim. In the 1775 Gorkha incursion, the Lepcha chief, Changzod Chothup, greatly distinguished himself, earning the sobriquet "Satrajeet". With Sikkim having the upper hand, once again Tibet played the role of the mediator and helped define the western boundary of Sikkim.

By 1780 the Gorkhas had pushed their boundaries up to the Teesta River, and Pemayangtse and the entire western region was paying taxes to Nepal, even forcing Chogyal Tenzing Namgyal, the sixth *chogyal*, to flee to Tibet, where he died in exile. However, the expanding Nepalese thrust eastwards under Bhim Sen Thapa brought them into direct military confrontation with the British East India Company. The Gorkhas were subsequently

Rabdentse Palace, today in ruins, was established as the second capital of Sikkim in the late seventeenth century by the second *chogyal*. Towards the end of the eighteenth century the Nepali threat necessitated a shift, and Tumlong came up as the next capital city. It continues to be an imposing site rich in the history of the growing prosperity of the Namgyal dynasty.

FACING PAGE
With the establishment of the first *chogyal*, the spread of Buddhism was undertaken and monasteries were built across the land. Sangachoeling Monastery at Pelling was one of the earliest, built in 1701. Located atop a hill amid thick forests, it is resplendent in prayer flags and elaborate Buddhist iconography. Its elevated position overlooks the Pemayangtse and Rabdentse ruins.

defeated in the Anglo-Nepalese War fought from 1814 to 1816 and the *chogyal*s were given back most of Sikkim after the Treaty of Sugauli. Tsugphud Namgyal was by then the seventh *chogyal* of Sikkim. While at war with the Gorkhas, the British treated the *chogyal* as an important ally, all the time eyeing future trade with Tibet through Sikkim. In 1817, the capital was shifted from Rabdentse to Tumlong for greater security. As a result, the Kagyupa monasteries of North Sikkim now came into prominence.

Having defeated the Gorkhas, British intentions became clear. After the Treaty of Sugauli, the Treaty of Titalya was signed, whereby the boundary between Sikkim and Nepal was delineated. This left large tracts of land still in the hands of Nepal, while the British retained previous Sikkimese territories around Titalya, which were acquired from the Gorkhas. This effectively reduced the *chogyal*'s influence to the river valley of the Teesta and the area east of the Singalila Range.

ABOVE | Pemayangtse Monastery stands at an altitude of 2,085 m (6,840 ft.) and was first built as a small temple in the late seventeenth century by Lhatsun Chhembo. It was later rebuilt during the reign of the third *chogyal*, Chakdor Namgyal, to its present eminence. The lamas of Pemayangtse invoke the blessings of Kanchenjunga during the Pang Lhabsol festival to protect the land and the people.

ABOVE RIGHT | Monasteries and *chorten*s are decorated with paintings that depict the Boddhisattvas, deities and saints in vibrant colours, images that have become a part of Buddhist lore.

In 1835 the British asked for and got Darjeeling from the *chogyal* as a gesture of friendship, at an annual rent of three thousand rupees. The Tibetan words *dorje*, "sceptre of the rain god Indra", and *ling*, meaning "land", made Darjeeling "the Land of the Thunderbolt". Crowned by the golden glory of the Kanchenjunga, clinging to the ridgeline at 2,045 m (6,710 ft.) in the Mahabharat Range, or Lesser Himalayas, Darjeeling is nostalgically referred to as the Queen of the Hills. The salubrious climate suggested an excellent place for rest and recuperation for officers of the East India Company. Over the years it transformed from an uninhabited hill to a British sanatorium and military depot and still bears the imprint of colonial times.

British control of the sub-Himalayan zone resulted in a major change in the demographic equation within the region. In the next hundred years, the entire socio-religious equation was to change dramatically. The development of Darjeeling as a British hill station saw the population of Sikkim virtually double in just the one decade between 1839 and 1849. Among its native population, Sikkim now could count the Magar, Newar, Gurung, Rai, Sherpa and Marwari, most of whom were attracted by the flourishing markets and the prospect of greater trade with Tibet. The British ushered in the Gorkhas, who were a martial race, and also inducted them into the armies to reduce the Bhutia-Lepcha majority. The initial Nepalese migrants into Sikkim were sharecroppers, who introduced terrace cultivation to the local populace. Even today they are mostly farmers. The Nepalese, who now outnumber the Lepcha and Bhutia, are themselves made up of different sub-cultural sects. The most important tribes are the Gurung, the Magar, the Limta, the Rai, the Tamang and the Mewar. They are mostly Hindus and the Brahmins among them are the Thakur and the Chhetri.

Sikkim was no longer in the mood to take the overbearing behavior of the British administration when in 1849 Joseph Dalton Hooker, a botanist and colleague of Charles Darwin, visited Sikkim. Hooker headed towards the Tibet border along with Archibald Campbell, where he was stopped by the Sikkim authorities. This perceived insult by the *chogyal* resulted in the British taking a series of punitive measures and by 1861 Sikkim was completely transformed into a British protectorate and the annexation of Darjeeling was confirmed. After the Anglo-Bhutan War, by virtue of the Treaty of Sinchula signed in 1865, the British gobbled up the territory held by Bhutan east of the Teesta River as well.

By the turn of the century, the focus had shifted to Gangtok, quite simply "Hilltop", standing resplendent at an altitude of 1,437 m (4,714 ft.). In 1894, Chogyal Thutob Namgyal made Gangtok his new capital. The trade between Lhasa in Tibet and Kolkata (then Calcutta of British India) in the early twentieth century transformed Gangtok into an important trade stopover. An integral part of the old silk route between India and Tibet,

LEFT | Looking for a place to meditate, Guru Padmasambhava shot an arrow that landed at Tashiding. Pedi Wangmo, Chakdor Namgyal's sister, built a monastery here in 1716 that is considered second in importance only to Pemayangtse. Replete with sacred *chortens*, the Tashiding hilltop stands between the Ratong and Rangit Rivers. It is said that every Sikkimese wishes to be cremated at Tashiding when he passes on.

Gangtok was the hub where yaks, mules and donkeys arrived laden mainly with wool, taking back in exchange salt, soap, precious stones, dried fruit and a host of other items. More than the trade itself, this economic flow influenced and shaped the entire dynamics of the region. Later with the sealing of borders, this trade died a natural death.

Becoming an Indian State

The two World Wars brought a sea change to the globe and India finally emerged an independent nation on August 15, 1947. In the immediate aftermath of Indian independence and the reorganisation of princely states, Nepal, Sikkim and Bhutan became the three Himalayan kingdoms that acted as a buffer between the two emergent Asian giants, China and India. At first, there was the standstill agreement signed between India and Sikkim to retain all previous treaties and agreements, while the people of Sikkim, inspired by the freedom movement, felt democracy was not far away. The 1950 Indo-Sikkim Treaty made Sikkim a protectorate of India.

ABOVE | Gangtok, the capital city, shimmering like a carpet of stars thrown over the hills. The city, its culture and its people bring together every strand of the life of Sikkim.

FACING PAGE
LEFT | The main market of Gangtok sees a never-ending bustle of tourists and local populace at any time of the day and way into the night.

RIGHT | The Police Band, popular with the young and old alike, plays a melody with all the sparkle of brass.

Fleeing from Chinese aggression in 1959 along with the Dalai Lama, the Karmapa also had to flee Tibet with his followers, who belonged to the Kagyupa sect. In order to preserve the lineage of the Karma Kagyu and the priceless treasures of the sect, Chogyal Tashi Namgyal invited His Holiness to Sikkim, and the Rumtek Monastery was constructed in 1962 to mirror the Tsurphu Monastery in Tibet.

Tashi Namgyal was a compassionate man, an artist at heart. He adopted measures to eradicate social evils and inequality. He was succeeded by his eldest son, Palden Thondup Namgyal, who, as the crown prince, had earlier led the Sikkim team that negotiated the treaty with independent India in 1949–50. After the death of his first wife Yapshi Phordang in 1957, the *chogyal* married Hope Cooke, the daughter of an American diplomat. This brought this hitherto "hidden land" into the gaze of the world. Palden

Thondup Namgyal was the last reigning *chogyal* and his reign witnessed major political changes that were to subsequently engulf Sikkim.

Since 1947 there had been an increasing demand for democratisation in Sikkim. After the furore between the Lepcha-Bhutia faction and the Nepalese majority over political representation in 1973, matters came to a head. The *chogyal* had to seek the help of India and thereafter the course was set. On April 10, 1975, the Sikkim Assembly passed a resolution demanding Sikkim be made a constituent part of India. In a referendum, 59,637 out of 61,133 voters, an overwhelming majority, endorsed the resolution. On May 16, 1975, Sikkim became the twenty-second state of the Indian Union. Since the arrival of the three lamas in Yuksom, the institution of the *chogyal*s had lasted for 333 years.

Two events perhaps also played a role in the merger of Sikkim with the Indian Union. Shortly after getting married to the *chogyal*, Hope Cooke, in a signed article published by the Namgyal Institute of Tibetology, questioned the legality of the grant of Darjeeling. This was seen by Delhi as a possible security threat as it was also felt that that the *chogyal* himself was leaning towards an understanding with China, under American influence. Secondly, during the 1971 war with Pakistan for the liberation of Bangladesh, there was a real possibility that China might enter the conflict via Nathu La and change the entire complexion of the war.

Since the merger with India, Sikkim has had five chief ministers govern the state, starting with Kazi Lendup Dorjee. The election of 1979 was the first election held under the Constitution of India. This began a process of the gradual integration of Sikkim with mainstream India. The Nepalese are Sikkim's most socially mobile community. Ahead in modern education, they hold important government posts and professional jobs, apart from being shopkeepers and tradesmen. An industrious people who live simply, they are dominating the modernisation of Sikkim. Economic mobility has somewhat rearranged the ethnic distribution, which earlier had the Bhutia in the higher alpine pastures, the Lepcha in the forests of the middle valleys, and the Nepalese in the lower valleys. Today most Sikkimese are fluent in Nepali and the educated conversant with English. The history of the three major communities in Sikkim somehow manages to bind the people together, each community having a deep respect for the other.

Assam

Assam, fondly referred to as "mini-India", is the heartbeat of the Northeast. At the northeastern tip of the state near Sadiya, the Siang River joins the Lohit to form the Brahmaputra, and the journey of this life-defining river begins, traversing the plains of Assam till it disgorges into Bangladesh at its southwestern tip, past Goalpara and below Dhubri. The Brahmaputra River rules this land, lending fertility to its soil and richness to its imagination, annually flooding and gathering up its waters, dictating the ebb and flow of life. A diverse mix of ethnic and linguistic groups like the Bodo, Bengali, Nepali, Mishing, Rabha, Karbi and others live in this region. Assam forms a kind of "T", wherein to the south of the Brahmaputra floodplains lies the region of Karbi Anglong and Dima Hasau, as well as the Barak River Valley, a distinctly different ecosystem.

In ancient times Assam was the Kamrup kingdom, taking its lineage from King Naraka who had defeated the Danav king. From circa 350 CE onwards, Kamrup rule was centred on the present-day Guwahati region. Three dynasties in succession—the Varman, the Mlechha and the Pala—dominated till the thirteenth century. Thereafter came the westward shift to Kamtapur into the Bodo and Mech regions. Central Assam saw

The Dibang River debouches from the hills and joins the Lohit near Sadiya to form the Brahmaputra. The deep valley to the north is thickly wooded and remained uncharted territory until the Morshead and Bailey expedition made its way to Anini and beyond in 1913. This survey was to form the basis of the McMahon Line that was drawn up in Simla the next year.

the ascendancy of the Kachari, and to the east the Chutiya ruled until the Ahom dynasties systematically established themselves.

The influence of Guwahati, Assam's premier city and the nerve centre of the Northeast, has perhaps been the single constant factor in a region where political changes time and again have altered the entire dynamic. Its geographical location, sandwiched, as it were, between the expanse of the Brahmaputra River and the mountainous region of the Shillong Plateau, allowed the city to control, protect and exploit the inner sanctum of the Seven Sisters.

Guwahati traces its origins, through mythical references in the *Vedas*, *Puranas* and other scriptures, to the semi-mythical town of Pragjyotishpura, founded by the *asura* King Naraka. Like most ancient cities of the world, Guwahati, by virtue of being on the banks of one of the greatest waterways, was an important cultural centre. Few cities on the planet would have seen so much change over millennia. Not surprising then, that Guwahati should evolve a character and ethos of its own—ranging from it being the seat of orthodox Tantrism and Saktism on the one hand, while also being the modern face of Northeast India on the other.

LEFT | The Brahmaputra catches the golden glow of the setting sun at Tezpur. In ancient times it was called Sonitpur—*sonit* in Sanskrit means "blood"—after Lord Krishna's army clashed with Banasura over the rescue of Aniruddha, Krishna's grandson. There was so much bloodshed that the whole place was awash in red.

BELOW | The symbol of the earliest Tai immigrants, the Ahom. Descendants of the Shans, they crossed the Patkai Hills from Burma in 1228 CE under the leadership of Su Ka Pha, and established the empire to which they lent their name—Assam.

The Bodo and the Ahom

The Indo-Mongoloid Bodo group of tribes, who settled in North Bengal, Meghalaya and Bangladesh and in some parts of Nepal, are the autochthons of the north bank of the Brahmaputra. They are a large number of tribes that speak Tibeto-Burmese languages. The "plains" Kachari, Chutiya, Garo, Mech, Koch, Rabha, Dhimal, Jaijong, Galong, Hojai and Moran are some of the tribes included within the larger community.

Today, the Bodo form the largest minority group in Assam, classified as "plains tribals" settled in the valleys, as opposed to the "hill tribes". They ruled over most of Assam in the medieval period, only to be later sidelined by the Ahom ascendancy and the subsequent British Raj. The main religious beliefs of the community are Bathouism, Hinduism and Christianity. Bathouism is a form of ancestor worship of the Bodo, known as *obonglaoree*.

During the decade of the 1980s the Bodo launched an intense and violent struggle to shake off the enveloping Assamese influence and pushed for self-determination. The political struggle by the Bodo for ethnic sub-nationalism is complex, in

that it has totally altered the cultural and economic structure of the state. The official Bodoland Movement, demanding the creation of a separate state, dates back to March 1987, when, under the banner of the All Bodo Students' Union (ABSU) there was a call to "Divide Assam Fifty-Fifty". Being one of the eight largest plains tribal communities of the Brahmaputra Valley, the movement slowly emerged as one of the biggest mobilised by any ethnic group.

This quest for political power has its deep roots in the lack of employment and developmental strategies in the region. Like other ethnic tribes, the Bodo faced severe land encroachment problems as individual holdings shrank for various reasons, including acquisition by moneylenders and the deprivation of forestland and resources, mainly through illegal methods. The initial demands for a separate homeland and identity started during the British period, when insecurities related to health, education and finance created widespread agitation within the community. The Bodo Sahitya Sabha was formed in 1952 and the All Bodo Students' Union (ABSU) in 1967.

Finally, in February 2003, the Government of Assam, the Union Government and the leaders of the Bodoland Movement jointly signed a Memorandum of Settlement in New Delhi enabling the creation of the Bodoland Territorial Council (BTC). Carved out of eight districts of Assam, the BTC comprises four contiguous districts, namely Kokrajhar, Udalguri, Baska and Chirang.

The Bodo language has a script of its own called Deodhai and it was introduced as the medium of instruction in all Bodo-dominated areas. A large number of biographies, short stories, children's literature and poetry were printed. On the economic front, also, the community has over time made a transition from shifting to settled cultivation. In fact, the Bodo have been credited with introducing rice cultivation, the original tea plant, poultry farming and silkworm rearing in the Northeast.

ABOVE | Bodo villagers, out as a group and armed with baskets, trap the small fish that are an integral part of their diet. The technique used is not dissimilar to that adopted by pelicans.

FACING PAGE
The Bodo are the original inhabitants of Assam, the autochthons of the north bank of the Brahmaputra. Classified as "plains tribals" who have settled in the valleys, as opposed to the "hill tribes", they ruled over most of Assam in the medieval period.

UNESCO World Heritage Site

Manas Wildlife Sanctuary

In the heart of Bodo country lies the Manas Tiger Reserve. It gets its name from the Manas River, which flows down from Tawang District in Arunachal Pradesh as the Gongri River, across Bhutan, where it is called the Drangme Chu, and finally into northern Assam as the Manas.

Compared to Kaziranga, the Manas Tiger Reserve is a much more secluded national park. The topography of the reserve is astonishingly diverse; the Manas River spilling out of the foothills, the sandy stretches interspersed with islands of trees, the forests of mixed deciduous vegetation and a mind-boggling variety of fauna—tiger, elephant, buffalo, hare, wild boar, primates, multiple species of deer and an incredible variety of birds. The area first shot into prominence when the planter-naturalist E.P. Gee reported the presence of the golden langur across the river in Bhutan.

Manas, despite its troubled past, has succeeded in protecting the hispid hare *(Caprolagus hispidus)* and the pygmy hog *(Porcula salvania)*, both of which were considered to be on the brink of extinction at one time. Manas had its own rhino population in the 1980s, but these were killed during the years of insurgency that followed. As part of the Indian Rhino Vision 2020 project, rhinos were translocated from Kaziranga, mainly with the objective of preserving the gene pool of the animal, which is otherwise mostly confined to Kaziranga today. The Manas buffalo has an impressive sweep of horns, as domestic animals have not been able to dilute the wild genes. The elephant in the region is equally distinguished, with most tuskers being much bigger than elephants elsewhere. Reports show that the tiger and other predators are also slowly making a comeback. Manas has a thriving insect, butterfly and reptile population. It is home to a breathtaking variety

of birds, ranging from minivets, bee-eaters and *kalij* pheasants to herons, eagles and pratincoles. It is a wilderness like no other and you leave with the distinct impression that if you had stood long enough amid its multifarious flora and fauna, maybe the forest would have claimed you as one of its own.

Bound by the foothills of the Eastern Himalayas and the north bank of the Brahmaputra, with the Sankosh River to the west and the Dibang River in the east, this is a 750-km (466 mi.) long area. It has an estimated 1,800 elephants and about 150 tigers. A nucleus population of about 40 rhinos is present in the Orang National Park. About a quarter of the area has the status of an elephant or tiger reserve. Elephants are concentrated in the northern areas, preferring the relatively densely vegetated foothills. However, disappearing migratory routes, due to the depletion of forest cover, have brought the herds onto the alluvial plains in search of food.

The steep topographical variation in the terrain also contributes to the rich biodiversity as different organisms specialise and adapt to different altitudes. The World Wildlife Fund has given the region a priority status as being one of the 200 global eco-regions of importance. Conservation International recognises the wider Eastern Himalayas as one of eighteen global biodiversity "hot spots".

Their range restricted between the Sankosh and Manas Rivers, the golden langur (*Trachypithecus geei*) is an old-world monkey, one among the most endangered species in the region.

ABOVE LEFT | Herds of Asian buffalo *(Bubalus arnee)* are usually seen in the grasslands. A solitary bull can sometimes be seen in the foothills looking to feed off cane and bamboo.

ABOVE RIGHT | The multi-coloured capped langur (*Trachypithecus pileatus*).

Photographs by Sujan Chatterjee.

FACING PAGE
Years of insurgency had severely impacted the wildlife in Manas. The Royal Bengal tiger *(Panthera tigris)* is now fortunately making a comeback.

The Ahom chronicles meticulously record Su Ka Pha's passage into India. His first domain was in the Kham-Jang Valley with the Nongyang Lake, which lies below the Pangsau Pass on the Patkai Hills.

BELOW | The art and architecture of the Ahom period is showcased in the monuments constructed during their extended rule, which marks the medieval period of Assam.

The earliest Tai immigrants, who originally belonged to the Southeast Asian region, into Assam were the Ahom. The 1891 census of Assam tells the story.

> The Ahoms, descendants of the Shans, under the leadership of Su Ka Pha crossed the Patkai Hills from Burma in 1228 CE, just around the time when Kublai Khan was establishing his power in China. They arrived at Somarpeeth from Mungmoulung, entering the upper portion of the province to which they gave their name, which later became Assam. Not being a large tribe it took them some time to consolidate their power. Prevailing over the Naga, Boran, Barahi, they were engaged for several hundred years in conflicts with the Chutiyas and the Kacharis. It was 1540 CE when they overthrew the latter, establishing their kingdom Mung-dun-chun-kham with its capital at Chareideo. In 1562 CE, the Koch king Nar Narayan, then at the zenith of his power, invaded their territory and inflicted a decisive defeat on them, sacking Chareideo.

Subsequently, the Koch kingdom was divided into two parts and saw the decline of its power and the consequent rise of the Ahom kings. The rajas of Jaintia, Dimarua and other kingdoms, who had been feudatories of Biswa Singha, the Koch king, acknowledged the suzerainty of the Ahom. Meanwhile, Muslim invaders time and again attacked the region unsuccessfully. In 1663 CE, the Mughal governor of Bengal, Mir Jumla, pushed eastwards with a large force. The historic river battle (unfortunately not so well known in the rest of the country) was the Battle of Saraighat that brought the troops of Mir Jumla face to face with the Ahom army led by the legendary Bor Phukan. Though initially defeated, the Ahom retreated yet kept up the fight, finally outlasting the Mughal forces. Thereafter, the victorious Ahom established their sway as far as Guwahati and finally reached as far as the Manas River, subduing all opposition along the way.

The Koch kings of Mangaldai and Beltola, too, accepted the suzerainty of the Ahom. The Ahom were now at the height of their power, all minor rulers acknowledging their supremacy, and even the Dafla, Miri and other hill tribes refrained from raiding them.

Towards the end of the seventeenth century the Ahom kings were drawn to Hinduism and they began taking on Hindu names

There were also two secret underground passages—a 3 km (2 mi.) connection to the Dikhow River and the Gargaon Palace for use as an escape route. The East India Company subsequently blocked this tunnel.

RIGHT | Originally, the palaces were constructed of bamboo and wood but brick, along with an indigenous type of cement, became the norm later on. Among the first brick palaces was the Kareng Ghar, built at Rongpur by King Rudra Singha (1696–1714). It was to become a seven-storeyed structure when three underground floors, known as the Talatal Ghar, were subsequently added.

alongside their Shan identity. Rudra Singh, alias Chukungpha, who came to the throne in 1695, had invited Krishna Ram Bhattacharya, a Sakta Gosain of Nadia, but passed away shortly thereafter. His successor, Sib Singh, became a disciple of Krishna Ram, who was established at the Kamakhya Temple. There followed increased dissension between those who had converted to Hinduism and those who had not, and the rift eventually led to the decline of the Ahom Empire.

The Ahom chronicles, or *Buranji*, are handwritten manuscripts passed on from generation to generation that chart their progress from when they fled from persecution in Burma to the arrival of many other Tai groups, including the Tai Khampti. All through their reign, the relations between the "hill people", as in the Arunachali tribes, and the Ahom were maintained through varied arrangements of reconciliation and persuasion. The *posa* system of paying tributes to keep tribes like the Nyishi, Aka and Miri from raiding the people of the foothills, and the policies of non-intervention and better trade opportunities worked well with the Mishmi, among others. Punitive expeditions, too, had to be undertaken, against tribes like the aggressive Dafla. The office of the *kotoki*s, or shield men, was used to negotiate with the tribal folk.

The Tai Museum at Sibsagar is one of the repositories of Tai history, especially the manuscripts that have been carefully handed down the generations. These handwritten documents deal with all aspects of life.

RIGHT | Sibsagar, the former nerve centre of the Ahom dynasty, is known for its shrines and temples. Shiva Dol is situated on the banks of the 200-year-old Sivasagar tank, also known as Borpukhuri.

ABOVE | According to the *Kalika Purana*, the Kamakhya Temple marks the spot where Sati used to retire in secret for an amorous tryst with Shiva. It was also the place where her *yoni* fell after Shiva danced his dance of destruction while carrying the corpse of the deceased Sati.

RIGHT | Kamakhya is the main Shakti temple in a complex of individual temples dedicated to different forms of the mother goddess, including Bhuvaneshvari, Bagalamukhi, Chhinnamasta, Tripura Sundari and Tara.

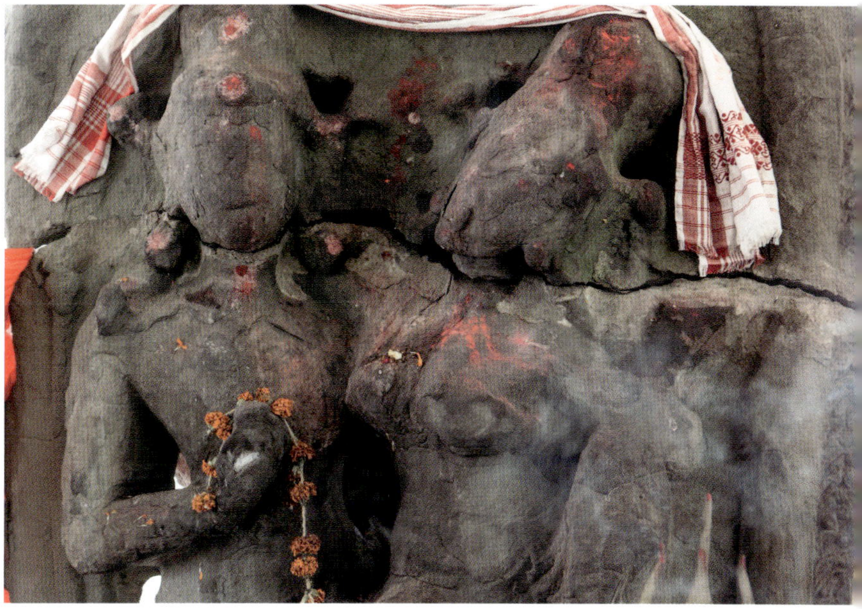

LEFT | Temple carvings where every surface is transformed by the sculptures timelessly etched on silent rocks.

BELOW | The Madan Kamdev Temple, dedicated to Lord Shiva, holds special interest for archaeologists as the ruins were undiscovered for many years.

Religion in Assam

Sibsagar, to the northeast of Guwahati and the former capital of the Ahom, is today known for its temples and shrines, chief among them being the Shiva Dol. Places of devotion and archaeological interest draw thousands annually. The most important pilgrimage site is the Kamakhya Temple near Guwahati. Hindu and Tantric devotees throng to Kamakhya during the annual festival, the Ambubachi Mela. The first reference to the place has been traced back to the Allahabad inscriptions of Emperor Samudragupta. The present temple, with seven oval spires topped by three golden pitchers, was built by King Nar Narayan of Cooch Behar.

According to the *Kalika Purana*, the Kamakhya Temple marks the spot where Sati used to retire in secret for an amorous tryst with Shiva. It was also the place where her *yoni* fell after Shiva danced his dance of destruction while carrying the corpse of the deceased Sati. Kamakhya is the main Shakti temple in a complex of individual temples dedicated to different forms of the mother goddess, including Bhuvaneshvari, Bagalamukhi, Chinnamasta, Tripura Sundari and Tara. The temple symbolises the fusion of faiths and practices of Aryan and non-Aryan elements in Assam.

The Madan Kamdev Temple, constructed during the reign of the Pala dynasty (10th–12th centuries CE) is dedicated to Lord Shiva, and holds a special interest for archaeologists as the ruins were undiscovered until 1977. The excavation revealed the ruins of around twenty temples, made of brick and stone. The sculptures captured the raw human emotions of fear, doubt, love, jealousy and passion. There are various legends about the temple, the most common being that Kama, or Madan, the God of Love, was reborn here after being turned into ashes by an angry Lord Shiva.

The famous Pao Mecca Mosque built in 1657 stands atop the Gaurachol Hills near Hajo on the northern bank of the Brahmaputra. Built by Pir Ghiasuddin Aulia, a foremost propagator of Islam in the region, *pao* means "a quarter" and the mosque is considered to have one-fourth the sanctity of Mecca.

RIGHT | Work on the Pao Mecca mosque began in 1657 atop the Gaurachol Hill near Hajo on the northern bank of the Brahmaputra. The mosque is considered to have one-fourth the sanctity of Mecca.

BELOW | Srimanta Sankardeva Tithi celebrations at a *naamghar* near Jorhat. Born in 1449, the poet-saint is the face of the Bhakti cult in Assam. Sankardeva integrated Assamese society, giving it a new concept and culture. *Naamghar*s and *satras* established by him are major socio-cultural institutions as well.

ABOVE | Open-bill storks are a common sight around monasteries on Majuli Island, their nosiy flights breaking the tranquil silence every now and then. Sankardeva established several *satras* within the physical boundary of the newly-formed island in the sixteenth century.

BELOW | Among the *satras* that have run the course of time and the effects of modernisation are Dakhinpat, Benegenaati, Kamlabari, Auniati and the Garamurh Satras. Each of the *satras* is famous for the distinct culture that it espouses.

Kamrup District today spreads on either side of the river. Along with agriculture, the district is also known for its raw silk production. The village of Sualkuchi has a plethora of looms producing some intricate *pat* and *muga* silk.

Centuries after the Bhakti cult, yet carrying the same reformist spirit, the poet saint of the Brahmaputra Valley, Mahapurusha Srimanta Sankardeva (1449–1568) integrated Assamese society, giving it a new concept and culture. "Ek Sharaniya Naama Dharma", a belief in one God and human dignity, became the cornerstone of the Vaishnavism he propagated throughout Assam. At that time, Hinduism in Assam was fraught with diverse cults, Tantrism and primitive occult practices, and was in a state of degeneration. The change he brought about was to inspire Mahatma Gandhi, centuries later, to say, "A great Vaishnava revival under Sankardeva has made the Assamese people kindly, tolerant and humane".

Majuli, India's largest river island, became the centre of the Sankardeva Mahadeva religious practice. A region of fluvial geomorphology, Majuli was formed as a result of the altered dynamics of the Brahmaputra River and its tributaries. In 1750, a massive flood split the Brahmaputra into two branches, with one part flowing along the original course and the other through a new channel called Dihing. The two branches later amalgamated, creating the island of Majuli, which subsequently became the centre of Assamese culture, especially with the spread of Vaishnavism in the region.

Sankardeva established religious training institutions like the Satras. There were 65 originally, but major floods in the Brahmaputra brought down the numbers drastically, so that only 22 of them remain today. Among them are Shamaguri, famous for the art of mask-making; Benegenaati, notable as a centre of performing arts and a repository of invaluable antiques; Kamlabari, which organizes cultural programs nationally and internationally; Auniati, which acts as a museum of ancient Assamese handicrafts and artefacts; and the Dakhinpat and Garamurh Satras, which are known for their elaborate *raaslila* celebrations.

When the British first entered the Northeast it was the Ahom kingdom that controlled the Brahmaputra Valley and was therefore the dominant power at the time. The Anglo-Burmese Wars that began in 1824, ended in a complete victory for the

When tea gardens began mushrooming all over the Northeast, 1874 onwards, the labour-intensive industry immediately faced a serious manpower problem.

FACING AND FOLLOWING PAGES
The word *bihu* is derived from *visuvan* that describes a number of Indian festivals associated with the March equinox. The Rongali Bihu celebrates the onset of the Assamese New Year and draws from many different traditions—Austro-Asiatic, Sino-Burmese and Indo-Aryan. There are two other *bihu*s: Kongali Bihu (mid-October) and the Bhogali Bihu (mid-January).

British. The Treaty of Yandabo, signed in 1826, gave them an unshakeable hold over Assam, Manipur, Cachar, Jaintia and other areas. British policy, either by design or otherwise, systematically made certain that the Ahom would henceforth remain a bit player.

The Famous Assam Tea

With the British started the story of the organised cultivation of tea. The Scottish brothers Bruce—Robert, who identified the plant, and Charles, who sensed the potential in this discovery—went on to become one of the first tea growers of Assam. The plant is indigenous to the region; in fact, prior to this discovery, the locals used to pluck the tea leaves and chew them. The original Bodo settlers are thought to have introduced both the tea and the rice plant in the region.

Today, Assam tea is a combination of the original type with the Chinese strain that early planters thought to be more valuable. But Assam tea is a sort of "stealth tea", mixing in with *keemun* and other black teas but always making its presence

known with its unique aroma, tart taste and honey notes. The most renowned Indian tea of its type, it is widely distributed across the world.

With tea gardens mushrooming all over the Northeast after 1874, the British tackled the shortage of local manpower for this labour-intensive field by bringing in a huge workforce from among the Adivasis of the Chotanagpur, Santhal and Pargana regions of Bihar and Orissa. People from far-off Tamil Nadu and Kerala were also tapped. Mostly Adivasis, these permanent settlers came to be known as the "tea tribes" of Assam.

The British brought in clerical staff in the form of *babu*s from Bengal and later made Bengali the official language of Assam. The growing dominance of the Bengali over the Assamese was further encouraged by allowing the influx of people hungry for land. The discovery of oilfields in Digboi at the turn of the nineteenth century, the first in Asia and only the second anywhere in the world, pitchforked Assam into its modern phase.

In May 1946, the Cabinet Mission that was dealing with the transfer of power from the British Government to the Indian leadership clearly underlined that Assam and Bengal should be combined to form a composite whole. By 1947, with Partition a looming reality, it took some desperate opposition from Gopinath Bordoloi to scuttle the British plans to make Assam a part of East Pakistan. Bordoloi received critical support from Mahatma Gandhi, who vehemently opposed the idea of looking at Assam and Bengal as one. The rest is history.

Assam's narrative continues in the major towns and cities like Dhubri, Goalpara, Dibrugarh, Jorhat, Tezpur and Sonitpur, as well as in the rural landscape dominated by large rivers and tea gardens, and in the remaining patches of forests among lush paddy fields where Bihu rhythms in intricately woven *mekhala*s continue to mark the harvest cycle each year.

UNESCO World Heritage Site

Kaziranga National Park

The Kaziranga National Park, spread across 430 sq km (166 sq. mi.) of grassland and impenetrable vegetative luxuriance, comprises close-tangled and thorny rattan cane, elephant grass and tall trees of the evergreen forests. Until 1908, Kaziranga was a trophy hunter's paradise, but the rapidly declining population of the Indian one-horned rhino forced the authorities, in 1926, to designate it a reserve forest. At one time estimates showed the rhino population reduced to double figures. The subsequent revival of this massive and powerful animal, reminiscent of prehistoric beasts, has been one of the more notable feats of faunal conservation in India.

The Brahmaputra overspills and ravages the surrounding area during the monsoons every year. However, once the waters withdraw, Kaziranga comes into its own, offering some of the best animal sightings. Kaziranga was declared a tiger reserve under Project Tiger in 2006. There are also large numbers of wild elephant herds present in the grasslands. In a group, they are usually fairly calm, but a solitary bull elephant can be a dangerous customer. The wild buffalo have suffered over the years due to interbreeding, resulting in the invasion of domestic genes. *Barasingha*, wild boar, hog deer, otters and lizards are other common sightings here.

LEFT | Cross-breeding with domestic buffalo, Kaziranga's herds have become feral. Earlier, herds of wild buffalo extended all the way up to the Lohit.

BELOW LEFT | Large herds of elephant can be found in the grasslands or feeding in the swampy *bheels*. In a group, they are usually fairly calm, but a solitary bull elephant can be a dangerous customer.

BELOW RIGHT | Kaziranga has a reasonable population of Indian hog deer (*Axis porcinus*) and the larger swamp deer (*Cervus duvaucell*).

FACING PAGE
ABOVE | A well-fed tiger is no threat to the swamp deer who eye the predator warily. Normally the big cats conserve energy, hunting only when they have to.

BELOW | A male *kalij* pheasant *(Lophura leucomelanos lathami)* breaks cover from the grasslands onto the jeep track.

Photographs by Dhritiman Mukherjee.

The reserve is also home to a vast assortment of birds such as the Assamese white-backed *kalij*, the red jungle fowl, the rose-breasted parakeet and the spot-billed pelican, among hundreds of other species. A personal favourite is the large swamp partridge, whose loud, insistent calls pierce through the morning stillness. Other rare game birds are the Bengal florican and swamp florican. Though the focus in the park is on the rhino and the elephant, the combination of grassland and dense vegetation houses around 478 species of birds, both migratory and resident. To this day, Kaziranga remains one of the few unspoilt floodplains of the Brahmaputra.

According to K. Ulhas Karanth, a senior conservation scientist with the Wildlife Conservation Society:

Ecologically, Kaziranga was a tiger paradise: the virtual absence of other large predators, such as *dhole* and leopard, which exploit the same prey species, ensured that tigers had a monopoly claim on the super-abundant prey base. Recent camera trap studies show that unlike many other places in India where tigers are in steep decline, they continue to thrive in Kaziranga. This is as much a tribute to the rigorous protection—originally put in place years ago by visionary foresters to save the last of the rhinos—as to the sustained social support the Assamese people give for such tough wildlife protection. Besides the rhino, the tiger as well as myriad other creatures big and small have been the beneficiaries of this conservation commitment.

DONATION BOX

WEST
Arunachal Pradesh

In the earliest reference made to this furthest tract of the Eastern Himalayas, the ancient text *Kalika Purana* calls it Prabhu Parvat, the "Mountain of the Gods". In the nineteenth century it passed through British hands as the North East Frontier Tract (NEFT), and after Independence this region was renamed the North East Frontier Agency (NEFA). Finally in 1972, when it became a union territory, the then Director of Research Bibhabasu Das Shastri re-christened it Arunachal Pradesh, "the Land of the Dawn-lit Mountains". The year 1978 saw Arunachal Pradesh take its place in the Union of India as a full-fledged state.

From time immemorial, the unending rugged mountains, the heavy and often unannounced rainfall, the thickly forested hillsides, the countless river valleys and the constantly changing terrain have been a challenge to its people. Add to this the remoteness of the region and its inaccessibility. Yet, throughout its history, time and again, tribes fleeing persecution or natural calamities, or seeking new land to occupy, have braved the high passes, entered the region and made it their home. Even as they battled the environment, the environment shaped them. For a long time the twenty-six major ethnic groups or tribes, with their hundred-odd sub-tribes, speaking over fifty dialects, had limited or no contact with the "outside world".

The 27-foot-high golden Shakyamuni Buddha dominates the magnificent *dukhang*, or assembly hall, in Tawang Monastery. Other precious possessions of the monastery include a silver casket containing the *thangkas* of Goddess Dri Devi, Palden Lhamo, believed to have been gifted by the Fifth Dalai Lama to Merak Lama, who founded the monastery. It is known as *ja-droi-ma*, meaning that it has the warmth of a bird, thus imbuing it with life.

West Arunachal borders the eastern flank of Bhutan, where the West Kameng District is home to the Monpa, the Sherdukpen and the Aka tribes. The region then extends further north beyond Se La into the district of Tawang, which is dominated exclusively by the Buddhist Monpa. The Nyamjang Chu, also called the Dargong River, originates at the northwestern extremity, where the borders of India, Bhutan and Tibet meet. It then flows south towards Lumla, where it is joined by the Tawang Chu, after which it enters Bhutan, flowing back into Assam in India as the Manas River.

The Anglo-Burmese Wars of 1824–26 gave the British a foothold that culminated in their annexation of the entire Northeast. The physical and political boundaries, especially those of western Arunachal, remained in a state of flux. In 1914, the frontier between Tibet and Northeast India was defined and NEFT was carved out from the Darrang and Lakhimpur Districts of Assam. NEFT at the time comprised the Western Section, the Lakhimpur Tract and the Central and Eastern Sections. Five years later, the Western Section was renamed the Balipara Frontier Tract.

Arunachal Pradesh had a population of around 1,300,000 according to the 2011 census, with the lowest density in the country, a mere 13 persons per sq km (around 33 people per sq. mi.). Today the state has seventeen census towns, with Itanagar being its capital city. Essentially an agrarian society, an overwhelming ninety-four per cent of the population continues to be rural, living in its 4,065 scattered villages.

Across Arunachal Pradesh, as the land translates from snow-clad peaks to rugged hillsides, the terrain is often spectacular. Here, a waterfall brings alive the rock face.

FACING PAGE
ABOVE | The Kameng River, earlier known as the Bhareli, graces the traditional route, descending into Assam from its glacial origin below the Gori Chen Mountain. Its frothing waters cover a distance of 264 km (164 mi.) before joining the Brahmaputra at Tezpur.

BELOW | Monpa houses, picturesquely perched on the hillside spurs, are substantial twin-storeyed buildings built on stone foundations. Each home is centered around the *medrang*, the family hearth, and a small chapel made of wood holds the family's divinities.

The Tribes of West Arunachal

The drive to Tawang starts at Tezpur. Barely 56 km (35 mi.) to the north, marking the entry into the foothills, is Bhalukpong, the gateway to Arunachal. King Bhaluka and his grandson Bana, from whom the Aka tribe claims descent, are believed to have ruled here in ancient times. The road cuts through the location of the Bhalukpong Fort, which doesn't exist anymore but in earlier times dominated the debouch point of the Kameng River (also called the Bhareli River). Recent archaeological findings of silver coins dating back to a Muslim ruler in Bengal indicate that Bhalukpong was the traditional route used to connect parts of Arunachal with the plains of Assam.

The hills dressed in pine, oak and fir are a riot of colour during autumn. The old trail to Tawang followed this route before the new road was aligned directly to Bomdila from Bhalukpong, via the Tenga Valley. It is contiguous with the Pakhui Tiger Reserve across the Kameng River to the east and the Sessa Orchid Sanctuary to the northeast. The Eagle's Nest and Sessa Ridges rise sharply from the plains to a height in excess of 3,048 m (10,000 ft.) and are the first barrier to the monsoon as it advances from Assam. One of Conservation International's biodiversity hotspot areas, the entire region is a wildlife sanctuary and one of the most spectacular birding areas in the world.

The two western districts of Arunachal, Tawang and West Kameng, are almost entirely Buddhist. In the Kameng region, the Sherdukpen are concentrated in the Dirang and Singte Valleys as also the Kalaktang (Bomdila) area. The Monpa were settled in the Tawang Valley when the first Tibetan migrants entered via Bhutan. Thereafter, they converted to Lamaistic Buddhism. They are subdivided into the Tawang, Dahing and Kolan sects. Their villages are characteristically dotted with *mane* walls and stone shrines called *chortens*. They are bound by a *pangchen*, or oath, to protect the habitat—this also means no hunting and no fishing.

ABOVE | The great Indian hornbill (*Buceros bicornis*), also known as the great pied hornbill, grows to an impressive size. It is often used in tribal rituals and worn as headgear.

RIGHT | The Indian eagle owl, also known as the Bengal eagle owl (*Bubo bengalensis*) inhabits the forests of the lower slopes extending up to 1,524 m (5,000 ft.).

ABOVE | Over 180 species of butterflies have been recorded in the Seijosa area of East Kameng.

LEFT | The golden-naped finch (*Pyrrhoplectes epauletta*), a denizen of temperate forests, is among a rich array of bird species, including pheasants, teals, partridges, waterfowl, warblers, and migratory birds like the Brahminy duck, mallards and an occasional white-winged wood duck.

ERFLY

PREVIOUS PAGES
A Monpa woman at her loom. This craft has been traditionally passed on from one generation of women to the next. From wool and cotton yarn to yak's hair; from loin looms to treadle looms to low wrap looms; from blankets, bags and even tents to carpets; from dragon motifs to flowers to snow lions to birds, this is a treasured craft.

The Monpa are one of the two tribes of Arunachal, the Tai Khampti being the other, who have their own script. They have preserved their Mahayana Buddhist scriptures like *Tanjur* and *Kanjur* in the Tibetan script. Their regional literature gives an account of the people, their religious activities and their earlier contacts with Burma and China. Tibetan chronicles record that the Mon people were once known to be a powerful kingdom. Tribal legend places a king, Gyalpo Kala Wangpo, at Tana Mandek Hong. Later, in the ninth century, the Mon king, referred to as the "King of Bamboo", was defeated by a Tibetan king.

Dirang Dzong, built in 1831, is situated half a kilometre (a third of a mile) from the town of Dirang. The Monpa of the Dirang Valley have several exogamous clans, or *khang*s, like the Faichurpal, Gunpapa, Baqipam and Shorthefa. Each clan has its place in a carefully maintained hierarchical order. The importance of this entire exercise was to regulate marriage so that there were no matrimonial alliances forged within the same clan. The family is the smallest social unit and the society is patriarchal and patrilineal, as are other tribes of Arunachal. The household activities of the family centre around the hearth, called *medrang*, which is normally in the middle of a long house. At the rear of the house is the courtyard, called *chosam*. Every family has a small wooden chapel in the shape of an altar in which are kept the images of several divinities. These are often ornately carved. The houses are substantial twin-storeyed stone structures perched picturesquely on the smallest of spurs, with terraces for cultivation cut around them. The Monpa women are known for their skill in weaving, which carries the stamp of Tibet and Bhutan, unlike other tribes who weave indigenous motifs only. Carpet weaving, with Buddhist and Chinese motifs, has been an important traditional craft. In Tawang and Bomdila, carpets and mats are sold as soon as they are woven.

The Monpa observe a clear class distinction and treat the Lishpa and Chugpa groups as social inferiors. Though similar with regard to religion and culture, their settlements are located at a distance from Monpa villages and they have their own dialect. The Monpa do not give their daughters in marriage to them. In fact, the Lishpa and Chugpa retain their identity and do not mix with the Monpa. The Monpa of West Kameng District, once again like the Tai Khampti, are one of two tribes with a written code of law to manage their political life. The village government is organised along democratic lines. The *tsorgen*, or village headman, is elected by the *tso-tsangom*, or village council. All

A man shows off the head of a yak. Conversion to Buddhism has resulted in some contradictory practices. The Kameng tribes forbid butchery, so yaks cannot be slaughtered but have to be pushed over a cliff to thereby obtain the meat.

FACING PAGE
ABOVE LEFT | A Sherdukpen youth out on a hunt. Hunts take place in groups with the help of dogs and poison arrows. The Sherdukpen fish by building dams across rivers with rocks, diverting the fish onto dry land where they can even be caught by hand.

ABOVE RIGHT | Traditionally, most structures and devices are built of stone. A young father, with a baby strapped to his back, is seen here pounding grain.

BELOW | The mountainous terrain makes horses and ponies the preferred mode of travel and for ferrying goods.

the villagers who contribute to the village fund are members of the council and are called *khreimins*.

Down below on the valley floor, the Tawang Chu makes it way eastward, where it is joined by the north-south-flowing Nyamjang Chu. The rivers are important migratory routes and lifelines around which the entire Himalayan belt has been settled.

Rupa is the area of the Sherdukpen tribe, numbering approximately 4,500 people. They are of Tibeto-Mongoloid stock, related to both the Aka and the Monpa and they are settled geographically between these two tribes. Rupa's history dates back to the seventh century CE and is related to King Tsongtsen Gambo of Tibet, from whom the upper class of the Sherdukpen claim descent. The *gompa* at Rupa, the largest and the oldest monastery in the Sherdukpen area, is believed to be 170 years old. It was also used as a fort where the people took refuge when their villages were raided by the Aka tribe. The *gompas* in the region are usually triple-storeyed, with elaborately painted prayer wheels and murals made by artists from Tawang.

Ancient Religions of West Arunachal

The belief that all true religions come from nature is upheld by most indigenous communities. Before Buddhism, the Sherdukpen, like the Monpa, practised a shamanistic faith with many gods and demons holding sway over the lives of the people. Essentially, this was similar to the Bon religion of Tibet. It is believed that in the eighth century Guru Padmasambhava destroyed the evil spirits and left many other imprints of his visit. Once Buddhism of the Mahayana school made inroads and became the accepted religion, the traditional sacrificial rites were abandoned. However, the indigenous spirits and deities found a place in the Buddhist pantheon as local defenders of the faith and continue to be worshipped.

A meeting of the Monpa village council in progress.

NIKE

Prepare for a journey.
Beyond the passes you'll need to go;
... till you reach our forest of conifers sprayed with snow.
That is our land, there are people there
Untouched by the Buddha's grace. They need a saint
And a monastery. Build a gompa there.

—The Fifth Dalai Lama to Merak Lama

A Sacred Space

With the words of the Fifth Dalai Lama, Nagwang Lobsang Gyatso, ringing in his ears, Merak Lama began a journey that brought him to this land of the Monpa. In a dream he had seen a white horse, agleam on a sunlit meadow, and sure enough, Tawang was where he found his own wandering horse, which refused to budge from there. All omens looked good. "This is destiny," he thought and smiled. "I'll build my monastery here, this is holy ground."

ABOVE LEFT | The ice sculptures that present Nature as an artist.

ABOVE RIGHT | Entire hillsides explode with colour as springtime spreads its warmth.

LEFT | The tranquil upper lakes at Se La that translate into fast-flowing rivers, slicing through the never-ending descent.

FACING PAGE
A gateway welcomes us to Tawang District as we ascend sharply to the Se La Pass. At 4,170 m (13,681 ft.) the rarefied air makes breathing difficult.

Morning prayers at the Khinme Gompa, with the head monk presiding.

FACING PAGE
The prayer hall resounds with chanting and music, while statues, paintings and murals from the Buddhist pantheon look on in divine benevolence.

FOLLOWING PAGES
The nuns of the Gyangong Anne Gompa, located barely five km (3 mi.) to the north of Tawang. There is a longstanding tradition of Anne *gompa*s, or nunneries, in Tawang. Unlike the boys there is no pressure on girls to join the nunneries and they do so of their own choice. But the Anne *gompa*s remain very modest affairs in comparison to the monasteries.

And so, in 1680–81, Merak Lama Lodre Gyatso founded the Gaden Namgyal Lhatse Monastery, whose Tibetan name means "celestial paradise on a clear night". The place and the monastery were more popularly called Tawang, meaning "blessed by the horse", as *ta* is Tibetan for "horse" and *wang* means "blessing". Standing at 3,292 m (10,800 ft.) above sea level at the northwestern edge of Arunachal Pradesh, it is the largest monastery of its kind in the country and the second-largest in Asia. Built on a spur, it commands a view of the Gudpi and Chong-Chugmi Ranges while the valley of the Tawang Chu lies below. Tawang is an important seat of Mahayana Buddhism, belonging to the Gelugpa school. It controls 17 *gompa*s in the region and is central to the spiritual life of the people.

Guru Tulku Rinpoche, the present abbot of Tawang Monastery, is recognized as the twelfth reincarnation of Lodre Gyatso. At the altar of the *dukhang*, the magnificent assembly hall, is enshrined the 27-foot-high golden Shakyamuni Buddha. Near the altar lies a precious possession of the monastery, a silver casket containing the *thangkas* of Goddess Dri Devi, Palden Lhamo, believed to have been gifted by the Fifth Dalai Lama to Merak Lama. It is known as *ja-droi-ma*, meaning that it has the warmth of a bird, thus imbuing it with life. Tawang has a long tradition of Anne *gompas*, or nunneries, as well.

During the 1962 War, Chinese troops had occupied the monastery, destroying some of its sections. In fact, China has made a claim to Tawang time and again, believing it can play an important part in the politics of Tibet, which remains under Chinese control since 1950.

Not far is the Khinme Gompa, which is the oldest shrine in the area and is the only monastery of the Nyingmapa sect in Tawang. The walls are covered with elaborate manuscripts and bas-relief on stones. This is an art form practiced by the Monpa, Memba, Khamba and Sherdukpen tribes. They paint on wood carvings, canvas and paper that then decorate the inner walls of monasteries, ceilings of domes and ceremonial gateways. The *kakalings*, or the hut-like structures at the entrance, are painted with murals showing the lives of Buddhist sages as well as Bon spirits that have been absorbed into the Buddhist pantheon.

Founded by Guru Padmasambhava, Nyingmapa is the most ancient sect of Tibetan Buddhism, also known as Lamaism. King Trisong Detsen, around the year 760 CE, invited Guru Padmasambhava and Shantarakshita, the abbot of Nalanda University, to introduce Buddhism to his subjects. They undertook the massive project of translating the *Dharma* from Sanskrit to Tibetan, the script and grammar of which was, in fact, created for this purpose. They also set up Samye, the first monastery in Tibet in 779 CE. The many lineages of the sect trace their origins to Guru Padmasambhava, popularly known as Guru Rinpoche, or Beloved Master, and worship him as the second Buddha.

Conflict at the McMahon Line

The monastic order of Tibet had always sought to establish control over the Tawang area. Despite the 1914 Simla Treaty clearly establishing the McMahon Line along the ridge to the north of Tawang, Tibetan intruders tried to extend their influence in the region. Persuasive assimilation, in keeping with the broad ethical ideals of Lamaism, seemed to have been the norm, though jailing defaulters was not uncommon. The Monpa

and the Sherdukpen resented the exaction of tributes and forced labour imposed on them by the Tibetans. In the Dirang area the Tibetans were in fact were known as *zakpa*s, quite literally, "plunderers". So when the British finally moved to extend their influence into NEFT in 1938, it was widely welcomed as the locals believed that the British Indian administration would not be as harsh and exploitative as the Tibetans.

In 1942 the Tibetan Government sent an army detachment to assert authority over the "Towang Salient", extending almost up to the plains at Udalguri. With World War II taking up all the attention, it was only in 1950 that Major Bob Khathing departed for Se La and Tawang with a small Assam Rifles detachment. Within six months, after a battle of attrition with the Tibetan intruders, he had wrested control of the entire area from the *dzongpen*s, or local officials, and established India's frontier with Tibet in accordance with the McMahon Line. During the same year, the Chinese annexed Tibet and stepped up their cartographic aggression against independent India by claiming almost the whole of NEFA. In response, the Assam Rifles formed the military vanguard taking the Indian administration right up to the border. New posts were set up all along the watershed. Matters came to a head in 1959. Tibetan refugees had been steadily crossing into India, the most famous being the Dalai Lama, along with members of his family, escaping from the Tibetan capital Lhasa and making for the Assam Rifles post at Chuthangmu. His Holiness was thereon escorted to Tawang, then Bomdila, Tezpur and Misamari and from there to Mussoorie.

It was on October 20, 1962, in the Nam Ka Chu Valley, below the Thag La ridge, that the Chinese first launched a major attack. What followed is history, with Indian troops taking a huge hammering. Designed like a Buddhist *chorten*, the memorial at Tawang is a testament to those trying days, carrying the names of all the 2,420 officers and men who were martyred there.

LEFT | Despite the demarcation of the McMahon Line, the Chinese attacked Bum La, among many other locations, in 1962.

RIGHT | The Himalayan blue poppy (*Meconopsis betonicifolia*) adds its own touch of translucent grace to the foliage.

East Kameng

Kangto Peak, locally known as Sher Kangri, is Arunachal Pradesh's highest peak, at 7,042 m (23,104 ft.). Flanked by Gorichen and Nyegi Kangsang, it forms the northern boundary of East Kameng District. This densely forested mountainous region is drained by three rivers—the Bichom (Humchu), Tengapani (Hudju) and the Kheyang (Khuwat)—which join the Kameng River flowing down from the east. Seppa, the headquarters of the East Kameng District, was earlier known as Salpa, or "marshy land" in the local dialect. It lies on the bank of the Kameng River, 160 km (99 mi.) from Itanagar. Seppa's communication network is extremely poor—the nearest airport is at Tezpur and the closest railway at Bhalukpong. The people of Seppa are either from the Nyishi, Sulung or Aka tribes. They are entirely agrarian and the introduction in recent decades of modern farming implements has helped them achieve greater productivity. Another significant avenue of income is pisciculture—apart from government fish-rearing farms, there are about 143 privately owned fishponds.

The northern part of the district is home to the Miji tribe, while the lower reaches house the Aka, who have been the dominant tribe in this area. In the past, the Aka were one of the most warlike tribes, with the Sherdukpen and the Khowa paying them tax. They also frequently raided and took on the British throughout the nineteenth century. The Aka are a small tribal group who call themselves "Hrusso". It is the Assamese who have named them Aka, which means "painted", possibly because they are known to paint their faces profusely.

There is an Aka legend that long ago all men descended from heaven to earth on ladders. The Assamese and the Aka of royal blood came down on a golden ladder, while the remaining (non-royal) Aka had a silver ladder. An iron ladder was used by the Monpa and the Tibetans, leaving the Adi and the Nyishi to manage with a bamboo ladder. They all descended to earth on Longkapur Hill in the Lohit Valley and then spread out in search

ABOVE | Aka women wear the long, red garment called *pol* and numerous colourful bead necklaces. A type of ancestral necklace, the *aeshesi* is worn invariably by women and often by men, too. The *aeshesi* is also gifted to girls at their wedding.

RIGHT | Flowers like the poinsettia exhibit a vibrant colour palette, much like the tribal communities resident here.

FACING PAGE
Life in an Aka hamlet combines leisure and work seamlessly on a quiet afternoon.

of land. The Aka spent so much time resting and drinking that the best land was already taken. Thus, they initially settled at Bhalukpong on the right bank of the Bhairali (Kameng) River, where their two chiefs, Natapura and Bayu, built their capitals. They also trace their genealogy from King Bana of Tezpur, a devotee of Shiva. They believe themselves to be descendants of Bhaluka, the grandson of King Bana. Interestingly, their migration, unlike that of many other tribes, is a south to north movement, from the plains of Assam into the hills.

They have two main divisions, the Kustum (Hazarikhowa) and the Kovatsun (Kapahchor). Their clan structure is patrilineal, with villages being owned by individual clans. Their social and economic well-being is dependent on the ability of the Aka to exploit the dense jungles around them for forest produce. Adept at moving through seemingly impenetrable vegetation, they are skilled archers—the bow is called *tkeri*, while an arrow is a *moo*—and also excellent trappers. An important custom among the Aka is that one of the sons stays on with his parents to take care of them, even after marriage. He then becomes the prime inheritor of the paternal property as the eventual successor. Some property passes to the other sons on marriage and ancestral ornaments are the prerogative of the daughters. The concepts of friendship and hospitality have a special place in Aka society as underlined by the traditional institution of *thumona*. The word means "guest", "guest chamber" or "visiting one another as guests". This brings the community together and creates a sense of bonding and belonging.

CENTRAL Arunachal Pradesh

> *"[T]he scenery, when it is not hidden by mist and rain, is superb; the people are charming, hospitable and photogenic: tribal institutions still retain their vitality. It is a country of song and dance, of hard enthusiastic work, of fine spinning and weaving, and of laughing, pretty children."*

The road to Tuting inspired these words from Verrier Elwin in the 1950s, which remain true even today.

From East Kameng to the Subansiri District, past the Ziro Valley, we come to the more recently formed Papumpare, where the capital city Itanagar lies. Beyond that is the spread of the Siang districts—the breathtaking stretch of central Arunachal Pradesh, with major tribes like the Nyishi, Tagin, Apatani and the Adi Gallong group, each dominating their zealously carved out territories. The Khemba and Memba Buddhist tribes of Tuting and Mechuka also take their place alongside the indigenous tribes of the Antagiri tradition.

Christoph von Fürer-Haimendorf first visited the confluence of the Kurung and Kamla Rivers, near Par village, towards the end of the Second World War. During British times, the Nyishi and the Hill Miri were referred to as "Daflas". Along with the Akas,

Ziro is one of the oldest towns of the erstwhile NEFA, the headquarters of the undivided Subansiri District. Nurtured carefully by the Apatani, surrounded by pine-clad hills, the valley is swathed in gold as the rice fields ripen in September and October.

they occasionally raided the plains of Assam, which in turn, lead to military expeditions into the area to "punish the tribes" as was the case in 1817 and 1830. Later, the terms "Dafla" (which had negative connotations) and "Hill Miri" were both dropped in favour of "Nisu" or "Nyishi".

The Tribes of Central Arunachal

Kurung Kumey District takes its name from the two rivers that drain it and Koloriang, the headquarters of the district, stands on the banks of the Kurung River. Spread across five districts in Arunachal Pradesh—East Kameng, Lower Subansiri, Upper Subansiri, Kurung Kumey and Papumpare—the Nyishi of the Kameng region are known as Bangni. According to Nyishi mythology, the first human being was born at a place called Korium Kolu, believed to lie somewhere within their vast geographical span. Atu Nyia being the first man on earth, they prefer to call themselves Nyeshang— literally, "descendants of Atu Nyia". The Hill Miri and the Tagin areas tend to merge and overlap with the Nyishi areas. Belonging to the Antagiri animistic tradition, but unlike the Adi tribes to their immediate east, the Nyishi do not have a name for their religion as such and their rituals and worship are more a way of life that is governed by nature. Their method of worshipping, called *weyi panam*, basically deals with spirits that are either antagonistic or benevolent. The universe is divided into three realms—*sichi*, the earth; *nyedo*, the sky; and *weyi nyoku*, the netherworld.

Their festivals are all a celebration of nature and are linked to agricultural phases. The five-day long pre-harvest festival Nyokum Yullo is celebrated for a bountiful harvest. It reaffirms ancient rites and rituals, binding the community together. The women in their traditional *kochik* and the men in colourful *pari* or *pomo aaje* outfits with the distinctive *bopia*, or headgear, present a dazzling colour palette. The Buya and Rikham Pada dances are performed with gay abandon. A *yugii*, or altar, is prepared and a ceremonial procession, *khome* or *tori*, is taken out.

"*Dola dola daiya hakin, dangla dagla hope pakin*" (When we get together, sit together, it strengthens our unity)," goes an

TOP LEFT | A Bangni woman. The Nyishi of the Kameng region are known as Bangni. They prefer to call themselves Nyeshang, or "the highlanders descended from the first man, Atu Nyia".

TOP RIGHT | Nyishi men wear a bun, called *podum*, tied with colourful thread. A pin of about twelve inches passes through the *podum* horizontally, holding it in place. The beak and feathers of the hornbill are used as adornment.

old Nyishi saying. The *nyejik*s or *nyegam*s (village heads) of the traditional tribal council, who are well versed in history, tackle socio-political problems. The process, referred to as *barek meta*, entails the taking up of any issue, relating it to events in the past, and arguing the case until all concerned are satisfied with the solution. This also makes the past a living issue in their present existence. Notably, among the Nyishi the status of women is extremely high—they are considered to be the source of peace, progress and prosperity.

Most Nyishi live in elongated houses in the Kurung Kumey area, each containing several families. As members of the extended household, it becomes incumbent on all members to support one another in the event of a clash with any outsider. The terrain also necessitated that houses be at a considerable distance from one another, resulting in tribe members evolving fairly individualistic traits. By the 1960s, starting at Yazali, the Nyishi had adopted wet cultivation and education was beginning to bear fruit. The number of students increased and they started involving themselves in social service and community work, helping to disseminate knowledge about the fast-changing world. These students also built roads, school buildings and community halls and played a major role in the adjustment and development process. Despite having lived in isolation for very long, the Nyishi today hold their own in virtually all walks of life, while strengthening their tribal identity.

Nyokum Yullo festivities are on in full swing and the women dance the Buya and Rikham Pada dances in their traditional *kochik* attire.

FACING PAGE
Seppa, the headquarters of the East Kameng District, stands on the banks of the Kameng River. Once a marshy land, it is now peopled with the Nyishi and Sulung tribes. It has a helicopter service linking it to Tezpur but this can be extremely erratic.

PREVIOUS PAGES
An "India bridge" spans the Kurung River. The Kumey River is considered the Kurung's sister, hence giving the district the name "Kurung Kumey".

RIGHT
A plentiful harvest brings smiles across Ziro.

In 1987 Arunachal Pradesh was declared the twenty-fourth state of the Union of India, and Papumpare District was carved out of Lower Subansiri later, with its district headquarters at Yupia. Itanagar, the capital city, traces its history back to the eleventh century when it was called Mayapur and was the capital city of the Jitri dynasty. King Ramachandra, alias Mayamatta, and his son Arimatta built Ita Fort, from which modern-day Itanagar derives its name, during the period from 1350 to 1450. However, a contrary view, based on recent studies of the Assam *Buranjis*, argues that the Ahom king Chakradhwaj Simha built the fort in 1688. The monumental and meticulously planned fortress covers an area of one square kilometre (one third of a square mile) and is believed to have been built using eight million bricks, or *itas*.

The two Subansiri districts are situated in the middle of Arunachal and have a combined area of 17,167 sq km (6,628 sq. mi.). The headquarters of Upper Subansiri are located at Daporijo, while Lower Subansiri is administered from Ziro, both among the oldest and more important towns of Arunachal. The history of the Apatani is without parallel among the tribes of the Northeast. Settled in the Ziro Valley, secluded from the outside world not only by terrain but also by warlike neighbours, the Apatani have marshalled and developed their resources in a manner that would do credit to any advanced civilisation. This is all the more remarkable, as they were a people using archaic and primitive equipment. Evidence suggests that the Ziro Valley was once a lake. The silt brought in by the streams helped fill up the Ziro bowl and provided the Apatani settled here with superior agricultural possibilities. The Apatani people have carefully nurtured the plateau on which the Ziro Valley is perched. Over the ages, they have evolved special agricultural methods best suited to optimize the growth of rice. They practise a uniquely successful form of rice and fish polyculture. Every step in the agricultural process has evolved in a special manner and, more importantly, been preserved over the ages.

Their settled lifestyle allowed them to keep their clans in close physical proximity to each other. Within the larger village, they followed a system wherein a clan village, known locally as a *lemba,* would be carefully segregated from other houses by an intricate system of bamboo fencing. Not only did this cement family bonds, it also allowed for the formation of a *patang*, a communal labour gang that provided the workforce to further evolve and hone agricultural methods best suited to their conditions. There is no particular chief or central authority in the village; instead the village council, called the *buliang*, manages day-to-day matters. Members are prominent persons of society and there is also a youth wing called the *ajang buliang*.

LEFT | An Apatani man wearing the traditional front knot, which is kept in place by the horizontal brass pin.

RIGHT | The traditional wooden nose-plugs once worn by the women are now seen less frequently on younger women.

BELOW | The Dree festival, the all-important Apatani festival, is held soon after the planting of rice.

In the immediate post-Independence period, venturing into the Subansiri area was left to the Assam Rifles at a time when India's own policies towards the tribal areas were yet to evolve. The Achingmori incident of October 1953 came as a shock—Major R.D. Singh, along with some political officers and 22 men from 7 Assam Rifles, was sent to investigate reports of Chinese agents operating in the region. The party was abruptly set upon by the Tagin, who killed all but three men and took most of the accompanying Gallong porters hostage.

The government refused to follow the time-honoured British method of dealing with such incidents, which would have meant "punishing" the tribes by burning their villages and other such depredations. Instead, troops were sent in the following year, the ringleaders were arrested and the Gallong porters freed. Interestingly for years after that, all Tagin met any query with the standard response, "I didn't do it! It was before my time." But outsiders remain quite wary of the Tagin temperament.

Tagin territory extends over 6,000 sq km (2,316 sq. mi.) across central Arunachal Pradesh. They are mainly concentrated in the riverine areas of Taliha, Syeum and Nacho and their land extends beyond Limking towards Taksing, from where Nah territory starts. According to myth the homeland of their ancestor, Abotani, is at a place called Sipa-Rigo near the source of the Subansiri River, while another myth traces their migration from Penji in Tibet to the junction of the Sipi and the Subansiri, ending at Siggen. The sharp valleys and relatively narrow spaces along the Subansiri make agricultural prospects poor, and the Tagin subsist on *jhum*, or shifting cultivation. They have a six-month lean period during which they survive by hunting and collecting roots and other forest produce.

The Tagin resemble the Adi in religious matters but are more like the Nyishi in social customs, traditions and their independent political system. Their society is divided into various classes—the priests, or *nibu*, and the rich, or *nite*, enjoy an elevated status in the community. They live in small villages with just a few houses built in the hollows of river valleys.

Daporijo town is settled on the banks of the Subansiri River. It is the headquarters of the Upper Subansiri District, a Tagin-dominated area.

The houses are elongated with several rooms for the numerous inmates and a separate hearth for each room. A Tagin house is a symbol of clan unity, with families under the same roof co-operating with one another. They are united against raids and inter-clan feuds, and like all *jhumming* societies, work together. Marriages are based on negotiations. The boy's father may send intermediaries to the father of the bride-to-be. Once the bride price is fixed, the marriage can take place. Polygamy is practised by the rich and cross-cousin marriages are accepted as a right.

The Tagin, like most central Arunachal tribes, believe in the Donyi Polo religion. Interestingly, they believe that a newborn has his or her destiny imprinted on the heart by *donyi*, the sun. Si-Donyi, the most important festival of the Tagin, is celebrated between the fifth and seventh of January each year. *Si*, the earth, and *donyi*, the sun, along with other natural elements, are collectively worshipped by the whole tribe.

The Nah people, a small community distributed across five villages, inhabit one of the remotest corners of Arunachal Pradesh, where the Subansiri River originates. They believe they are the descendants of "the mother of rain". Another popular legend claims that four brothers, two of whom were called Niye and Nije, came across the great mountain wall from Tibet. The Nah people are said to be descendants of Niye, while Nije's progeny are the Bangni. Life is very much at a subsistence level. They practice Mahayana Buddhism and Taksing is a pilgrimage centre.

Rich sculptural and archaeological remains were unearthed or reclaimed from the surrounding forest in 1968, in the foothills of the Abor (Adi) Hills in West Siang. These were the Malinithan temple ruins dating between the tenth to twelfth centuries, revealing not only the presence of Hinduism in this region but also its strong linkages with the mainstream culture of the country.

PREVIOUS PAGES
A Tagin couple returning from a foray in the forest.

The Goddess Malini, sculpted from granite, presides over the temple of Malinithan.

Malinithan rests on a hillock not far from the Brahmaputra River in Likabali. Mythology places it as part of the legend surrounding the marriage of Lord Krishna with Rukmini, the daughter of King Bhismak of Bhismaknagar nearby. Krishna set out for Dwarka with Rukmini, stopping to rest where Lord Shiva and Durga (Parvati) were in meditation. Durga made garlands of flowers for Rukmini and such was their beauty that Krishna gave Durga the name Malini, meaning "she who makes beautiful garlands". The *Kalika Purana* speaks of Akashi Ganga, located seven km (4 mi.) above Malinithan, as a *pithasthan*, or pilgrimage centre. The reigning deity of Malinithan that brings it into the Shakti pantheon, like the Kamakhya Temple in Guwahati, is the ten-armed Shakti Durga, or Mahishasuramardini, in Katyayani form. Sculpted in granite, she is worshipped as Goddess Malini, who destroys Mahishasura in the *tribhanga* posture, while standing on her *vahana*, or mount, which is a lion.

Entering India at Gelling, the Siang River, with its heaving magnificence, is the only "male" river of our country. During early geographical exploration it was considered to be the "missing link" between the Tsang Po of Tibet and Assam's Brahmaputra. Much later it was revealed to be the very same river. In Tibetan cosmogony, it is the "Horse Mouth" River for those who drink from it become as strong as a horse. A land of deep gorges and fast-flowing streams, the lower and upper reaches of the Siang are the domains of the Adi peoples. Earlier known as the Abor, the Adi, quite literally, "hill or mountain tops", are actually several tribes united by a similar language and culture. They are grouped into two sets of communities based on where they live. The Minyong, Padam, Shimong, Milang, Pasi, Karko, Pangi, Tangam and Bori belong to eastern Siang, while the Gallong, including the Ramo, Pailibo and the Bokar, occupy the western regions. During the British period the entire Siang region was referred to as "Abor country". The warlike qualities of the Abor rattled the British and there were several clashes between them. In the immediate post-Independence period the Assam Rifles played a major role in opening up the area.

The Nah Tagins of Taksing in celebratory mode. Taksing is a four-day walk from the road at Limking and life is very much at subsistence level but festival time brings out all the vibrancy of tribal life.

LEFT | Once known to be home to a very violent people, since the 1960s the Ramo and Pailibo region has become a "very friendly part of the world," as noted by Verrier Elwin.

FACING PAGE
A Bokar man from Monigong, to the northeast of Mechuka, wears the trademark cane hat.

Mechuka

The original Khamba tribe inhabits the area around Gelling and the Yang Sang Chu, or Yonggyap Valley, near the Tibetan border. Guru Padmasambhava is said to have brought them into the fold of Mahayana Buddhism and they are considered ethnically akin to the Monpa of the Kameng District. Almost each village has a *gompa* that is presided over by a lama. The name "Khamba" also refers to Tibetans living in Kham. They are culturally advanced in comparison with other tribes. Both the Khamba and the much smaller Memba tribe practise terrace agriculture, and they were the only communities in the region who were familiar with the art of fabricating water mills. Water-propelled grooved wooden blades worked grinders that crushed grain. In each village these mills were a common feature.

Mechuka, known as a "hidden heaven", is home to the Memba, the third-largest Buddhist tribe in Arunachal Pradesh, who migrated east from the Tawang Valley centuries ago. Like the Monpa, they too are deeply religious and virtually every aspect of their life is moulded by religion. Buddhist prayer flags called *phan*s are seen outside all Memba homes. Mantras are inscribed on them so that they purify the air as the wind scatters the letters of the mantra.

Despite being Buddhists, the Memba continue to worship some of their pre-Buddhist animistic deities. Their faith is a mix of two different cultures. While espousing the values of *ahimsa*, they think nothing of performing animal sacrifice to propitiate sundry traditional spirits. The Memba have been quick to adapt to outside contact, and when the Ramo first appeared at their doorstep two hundred years ago, they allowed them to settle on the fringes of the Mechuka Valley.

The name Mechuka derives from the Tibetan *me* "medicine" + *chu* "water" + *kha* "mouth of snow". The valley is also known as Banja Shingri, or "Hidden Heaven". The Samten Yongcha Gompa overlooking Mechuka town has cast its benevolent presence over the lives of the people—from daily chores to festivities and celebrations—since the middle of the seventeenth century.

By 1971 almost all the Siang tribes had prefixed "Adi" to their tribe name, regardless of ethnological considerations. The reason for this may well have been the desire to find a larger tribal identity in the region. The life of the Adi maybe lived entirely in their hill villages, each complete in itself with its *gaon burra*, who moderates the village council, which also acts as the traditional court, or *kebang*. All the village elders are part of the decisions taken by a majority verdict in a *dere*, as the community house is locally known.

These Indo-Mongoloid tribes do not have any written scripts, and a gifted orator, known as the *kebang abu*, usually traces the origin and migration of the Adi people from Uli, Usha and the Kumting regions of Tibet. During festival days, on occasions like Mopin, Solung, Dree and Nyokum, the *abu*s trace the entire cultural life of their people by reciting a long poem. Special rhapsodies, known as *abang*s, chart the course of the myth of creation, the origin of social institutions, and the history of the people. *Ponung*s are long ballads that recount the origins of a range of things. Usually, the formal introductory speech made by the *abu* also speaks of the political aspect of tribal life.

The central focus of the deep-rooted faith of the Adi religion, Yelam, are the two supreme beings Donyi, the sun, and Polo, the moon. They are the material manifestations of the Almighty, they are omnipresent, omniscient and omnipotent and forever vigilant. There is an Adi saying, "*Donyi mikmi seri ne; Polo migo sero ne*", meaning that the searching and piercing eternal eyes are ceaselessly watching humanity. Therefore, much importance is attached to a man's conscience. "Be truthful and honest, everything else will follow." Love and compassion, purity and wisdom, selflessness and tolerance, justice and equality, are the

hallmarks of a man of virtue. Donyi Polo is in essence the natural and spontaneous expression of Tani spirituality. It is a way of life that has evolved as nature worship, an interpretation of spirituality emerging from their experience of life.

Along, the headquarters of West Siang, is one of the oldest and most important towns of Arunachal. With the expansion of educational opportunities have come social transformation and a better quality of life—Along reflects the modern face of a self-confident state. But the relationship of tribal people and the plant world continues to evolve. Daily life involves all members of the family preparing for meals by heading off to the jungle with the *dao* in hand, prising and collecting all manner of roots, shoots, ferns, moss, seeds and flowers.

The Adi Gallong homeland is west and southwest Siang, along with their sub-tribes the Bori, Pailibo, Bokar and Ramo. Though completely interdependent for their survival, all the tribes have zealously preserved their identity, name and status and insist on being addressed by their ancestral names. The Galo trace their origin from Jimi, the Creator who brought forth *mrdo*, the sky, and *sichi*, the earth, which brought forth Tani, the first man who became the common father of all the tribes. They feel that the power that coordinates and harmonizes the existence of the universe is drawn from nature and its imprint is seen everywhere and in everything. The concept of Donyi Polo is the first realization of nature's vital role in their lives. All the *uyo*s, or rituals, performed to importune benevolent forces and ward off evil spirits invoke the power of nature.

Mopin is their festival of germination, preservation and true worship of Mother Nature. The Galo believe that when Tani came of age, he performed an *uyo* to Mopin with the help of the two goddesses Pinku and Pinte. The pleased Mopin showered Tani with all varieties of food grain. *Apong*, rice beer, is distributed, animals are sacrificed and feasts are held. *Ette*, or rice flour, is applied to one another in revelry and women do the traditional Poppyir dance in a month-long celebration. *Apong* is drunk on just about every occasion and in huge amounts during the Mopin festival. The preparation is a three-month long process—the rice is dried, smoked, fermented, filtered and then drunk out of bamboo flutes.

The Gallong live in joint families with their houses located preferably on high spurs. They are expert hunters and the post-harvest dry season is, traditionally, the time reserved for hunting. The entire village gets together in the *moshup* and organises the collective hunt. The Adi use traps of various kinds for bigger and smaller animals. They claim the right to all the fish in the rivers flowing through their areas. The tribe was famous for the cane bridges that they built to ford their countless streams, even the mighty Siang. Crossing these bridges is a nerve-wracking experience! Today, cane has been replaced by steel wires and these suspensions across rivers are locally known as "India bridges".

Children of the Bori tribe peep out of a hamlet at passers-by on the Mechuka-Along road.

FACING PAGE
A priestess leads the rituals of Donyi Polo worship that are very much a part of daily routines.

Their political structure is three-tiered, starting with the *kebang*, or village council, after which comes the *bango*, or inter-village council, and at the top is the *bogum bokang*, or the divisional council. Despite the difficult terrain and the lack of communication facilities, the other Adi tribes around the Gallong have taken tremendous steps to keep in touch with the demands of modern society. After the advent of Panchayati Raj, the Bokar, along with the Ramo, became politically very aware, taking a keen interest in self-government and also combining with the other tribes to contribute leaders who went onto serve the state. Tadik Cheese was a Bokar who became the deputy speaker of the Arunachal Pradesh Legislative Assembly in the late 1970s.

The confluence of the Siyom and the Siang at Pangin village in East Siang District is the main territory of the Adi Minyong tribe. They inhabit both banks of the Siang, from the Tuting area to the plains of Assam. The Minyong stubbornly resisted British attempts to subjugate this region. After spreading through Assam, the British pursued a policy of coercion and conciliation while slowly penetrating the hill areas. This was strongly resented and the Minyong were determined to protect

ABOVE | A young Adi Gallong woman's smile reflects the self-confident, modern face of Along, or Aalo, the headquarters of West Siang District.

RIGHT | The broad expanse of the valley where the waters of the Sipu River flow into the Siyom is the setting for Along.

Trophies from assorted hunting trips are proudly displayed on the walls of this hut.

RIGHT | Heading off into the surrounding jungle, the ever-present *dao* is put to effective use, prising out and collecting all manner of ferns, shoots, roots, berries, moss, seeds, and flowers. Arunachal Pradesh has well over 500 species of medicinal plants among its myriad plant forms.

FACING PAGE
The Pangin village of the Adi Minyong tribe.

their rights to the land and to the forest, and so the Abor tribes closed ranks. Like the freedom movement raging in the rest of the country, the Adi throughout tried to prevent colonisation at all costs. The areas beyond Yingkiong, towards the Dibang Valley, still remain relatively unexplored. The Adi Bobum Bokang, the Adi Ashing, the Adi Tangam and the Adi Shimong are spread across the Tuting landscape.

As we leave this area we revisit the "riddle of the Tsang Po gorge", one of the world's biggest geographical mysteries. The Tsang Po originates in the Chemayungdung glacier at the Tamchok Khambab Chorten, flowing eastwards on the northern side of the Himalayan watershed along the Tibetan Plateau. Close to Lhasa the river was at an altitude of 3,658 m (12,000 ft.) but further to the east, as it approached the Namcha Barua massif, it seemed to disappear. It was only in the early twentieth century that the British explorers Bailey and Morshead confirmed that the Siang was indeed the Tsang Po. However, it was left to Kingdon-Ward and Lord Cawdor to actually penetrate the precipitous gorge of the rumoured "Falls of the Brahmaputra" in 1924–25. Within Indian territory, the Siang, also referred to as the Dihang River, flows in a north-south direction and forms the nucleus of the dendritic drainage system of the Himalayas. Various subsidiary rivers—Shimang, Yamne, Siku, Sibia, Ringong, Sigang, Nidyang and finally, the Siyom that joins it at Pangin—add substantial volumes of water to the mighty Siang. After it enters the plains at Pasighat, the river joins the Lohit that has already merged with the Dibang. And the story continues...

EAST
Arunachal Pradesh

Matai, the supreme god of the Mishmi, thought of making a beautiful world in which the living and non-living would exist in interdependence, linking everything seamlessly. So at first he created human beings out of rock and metal but this was a failure, as they had no feelings. Matai then used mud and soil and the human forms were far more sensitive and could be moulded. He created Jim and Janey, one masculine and the other feminine, from whom all people are descended, or so say the Miju Mishmi. Incidentally, the three Mishmi tribes do not refer to themselves as Mishmi. The Miju are "Kmaan Jhaow" to the Digaru, who, in turn, are known as "Tah-wrah" or "Chimmu" to the Miju. The Idu are referred to as "Mindow" by the Miju and "Daiye" by the Digaru. You can take your pick as suits the moment!

In 1913 the area north of Anini was explored, photographed and mapped by two British officers, Colonel F.M. Bailey and Captain H.T. Morshead, who first went up to Andra La, then turned back and proceeded up the Mathun Valley to Yonggyap La, which they estimated to be at 3,664 m (12,020 ft.). Having crossed over into Tibet they then proceeded westward towards the Brahmaputra gorge, finally returning to India in the Tawang region. During this epic journey they undertook a detailed survey of the terrain, climbing several important landmarks to take readings. These findings formed the basis by which Sir Henry McMahon later

The Adi of Dibang Valley celebrating Indigenous Faith Day along with the rest of the state with traditional fervour and gaiety.

drew his line along the Himalayan watershed, demarcating the boundaries between British India and Tibet during the Simla Conference in 1914.

Perched on the Aninese Plateau, flanked by the Dibang and Mathun Rivers, lies Anini, headquarters of the Upper Dibang District. It is sparsely populated, with poor road communication. Its local name, Innini, in all probability originated from the Idu Mishmi word *inni*, meaning "supreme deity" or "god". We were met at the helipad by Idu priests and women dressed in their traditional attire. Almost every individual made it a point to thank us for having taken the trouble to get to their location, which they proudly pointed out was the northernmost district headquarters in the entire Northeast.

To the immediate east of Anini lies the Dri Valley, which has three major passes, all of them on the McMahon Line. The northernmost is the Adzamkho La. To its southeast lies the Tsang Khang La, at one time a popular route connecting to Zayul in Tibet, used by the Idu Mishmi to barter animal skins and red salt with the Tibetans. This pass is said to have been cursed by a Tibetan lama to keep the Idu Mishmi from stealing their chickens, so a third pass to its north was used—Aguia La. These passes fall in the region marked as Fishtail 1 on the map, an area which is completed uninhabited.

At Anini, an Idu Mishmi priest on his way to the Reh festival welcomes us to this northernmost district headquarters in the state.

The Mishmi Hills span the five easternmost districts of Arunachal Pradesh—Lohit, Anjaw, Upper Dibang, Lower Dibang and Upper Siang. These districts are peopled by the Miju and Digaru Mishmi, who are very similar in culture, rituals, dress and lifestyle, except for the dialect. The Idu Mishmi share certain rituals, marriage and administrative customs and have somewhat similar hunting and fishing techniques as the other two groups. The Mishmi were first encountered by the British when, in 1825, Lieutenant Burton of the British Indian Army came across them while exploring the upper tributaries of the Brahmaputra beyond the Nao-Dehing. They were observed to be aloof and distant and not very forthcoming with strangers. Their interaction with the British steered clear of appeasement or allegiance. When the international boundary was demarcated, some parts of the Mishmi homeland became parts of China and Myanmar.

Though the Upper and Lower Dibang Districts are known to be dominated by the Idu Mishmi, the settlements in the plains, especially the Roing and Dambuk areas, are Adi-dominated, among which the Padam are the major Adi tribe, in addition to Milang, Komkar and the Balak. The Padam have a rich cultural and oral

LEFT | The Yonggyap La Pass, at 3,664 m (12,020 ft.), is seen in the foreground. The distant Namcha Barua Peak, which the Tsang Po circumvents on its way to becoming the Brahmaputra, stands across the border, 50 km (31 mi.) inside Tibet.

BELOW | A detailed exploration, survey and mapping along the NEFA watershed undertaken by Colonel F.M. Bailey and Captain H.T. Morshead, which established the height of many important landmarks, was to become the basis for the demarcation of boundaries known as the McMahon Line.

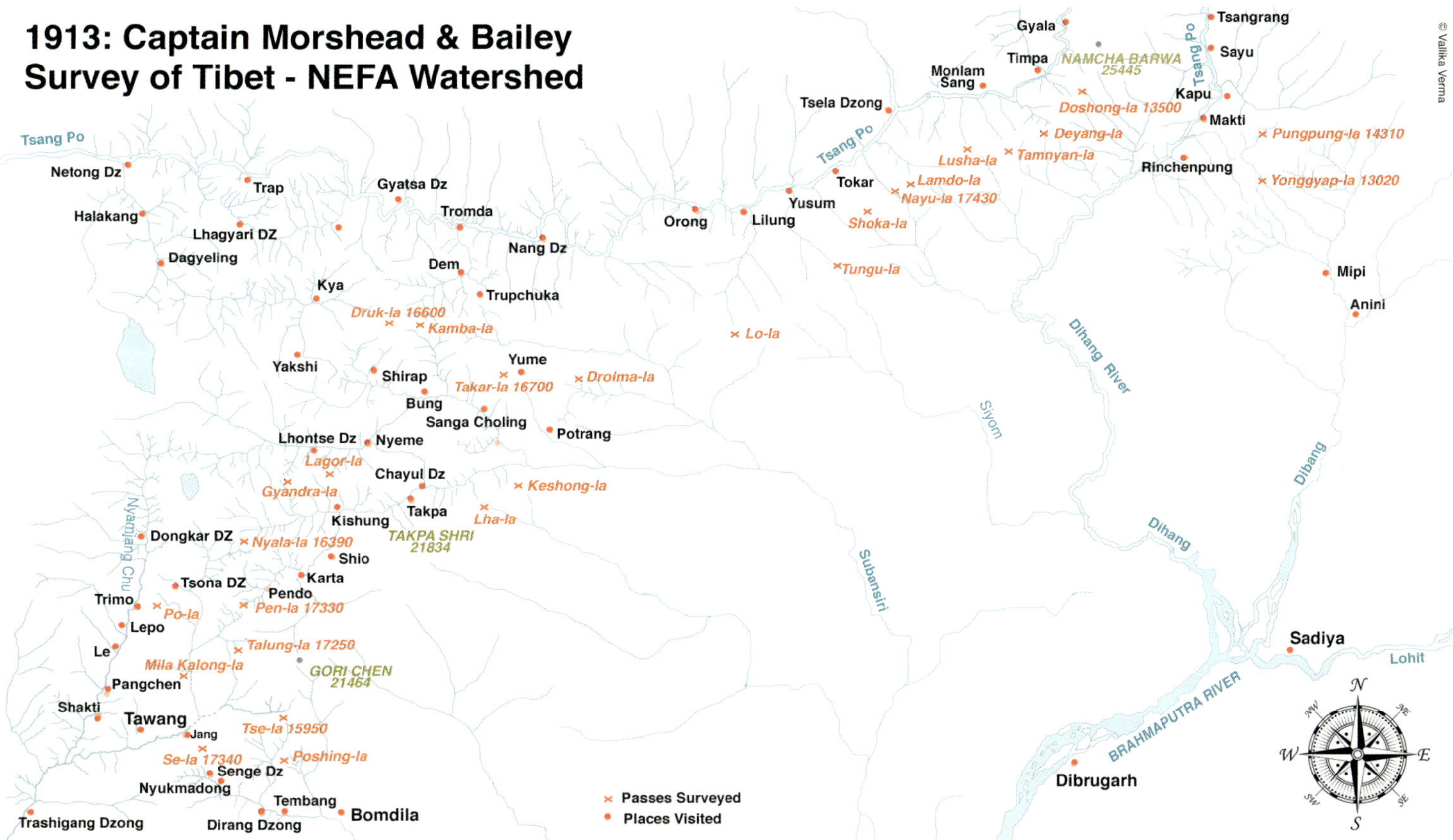

A much-welcomed hot meal being prepared in the lone "hotel" at the Mayodia Pass, standing at 2,652 m (8,700 ft.), 56 km (35 mi.) from Roing. From Mayodia, the snow-clad mountain range to the northeast separates the region from Anjaw District.

BELOW | The beautiful women of the Idu Mishmi tribe, resplendent in their beads and weaves that would be the envy of the faraway urban world!

FACING PAGE
Song and dance all the way to Roing for the Reh festival in February!

tradition that speaks of a vibrant society which functions on strong democratic principles and a sense of community. Their desire to occupy more land, supported by fierce war tactics, has given them a relatively aggressive reputation.

The Adi, as a whole, are considered to be far more advanced in comparison to all the other tribes of Arunachal. The Dibang Adi are agriculturists, engaged in both wet rice and shifting cultivation. They have an abundant growth of cash crops like maize and mustard, and are economically self-sufficient. The villages are surrounded by jackfruit trees and the houses are arranged in rows, leaving a fair amount of space for passages and emergency scenarios. Granaries are placed at the outskirts of the village to reduce fire hazards. At the centre is the *dere* or the *moshup*, the village council hall from where the *kebang* functions. A *moshup* site is selected with a commanding view of the various approaches to the village. It is also the bachelors' dormitory, while young unmarried girls have their own dormitory, the *rasheng*. These time-honoured institutions have contributed richly towards the welfare of the tribe. They are excellent training grounds for the individual, also regulating sexual and matrimonial relationships in Adi society.

Among the Adi the *rutum*, or nuclear family, is the smallest family unit. After marriage the elder siblings set up home independently, while the younger one stays back to take care of the parents. It is also not uncommon to find two or more kinsmen sharing a house. The seniormost male member is the head of the extended family and the eldest son is the primary inheritor. Monogamy is the norm but polygamy is also known, each wife having a separate apartment. Ideally, marriages are arranged and arrived at by negotiation. Women are also free to choose a life partner and "love marriages" are quite popular. Like most tribes of Arunachal, the Adi have the custom of bride price. An exchange of gifts by both the parties starts with the finalisation of negotiations and is called *apong kadung*.

Religion and Festivals in East Arunachal

Early February is the time for the Reh festival in the Lower Dibang Valley and all roads lead to Roing as the Idu Mishmi get into their annual celebration mood. Women holler out the traditional Idu Mishmi greeting "Meye-bo!", which is repeated in chorus whenever an honoured guest appears for the first time. "They dance with *mithun* blood!" scream websites that promote the event, in the belief that the more macabre the

FOLLOWING PAGES
Cooking together as a community is a very enjoyable part of the five-day festivities.

better! Myth has it that Reh was started by a slave named Apiju. In 1968, legendary social reformer Naba Ita Pulu made it an annual festival, bringing families and the community together, symbolising the unity, integrity and fraternity of Idu Mishmi society. Reh is traditionally performed with many ritual offerings and sacrifices made for the wealth and well-being of the family.

Andropu, the first day of the five-day festival, starts with the *igu*, or priest, performing rituals for the well-being of all the guests, the *meye-aji*. This is the day when everyone arrives and gifts are exchanged; there is a feast and a dance competition at night. The next day is Eyanli, when, early in the morning, the *mithun*s are sacrificed. On the third day pig sacrifice is ordained. On Iliru-muni or Aru-go, the fourth day, a highlight of the festivities is the mocking dance by the *igu* that causes much hilarity. The god known as Apessa is propitiated to grant a bumper crop and prosperity. On the concluding day, Etonu-che, fowls are sacrificed in the morning and distributed among one and all. Community bonds are revived and traditions kept alive as the Idu Mishmi, young and old, gather annually to make this one of the most spectacular festivals of the region.

The Mishmi religious system is animistic and the shaman, known as *kambring* or *gwak*, plays a vital role in handling spirits both benevolent and malevolent and removing obstacles to the prosperity of the individual, society and even the environment. Their religious observances have evolved from placation, avoidance, exorcism, coercion, conciliation and propitiation to sacrifice, atonement and redemption.

Situated 24 km (15 mi.) east of Roing, at the end of a long walk, one finds the remnants of a wall glimpsed under a shroud of green secrecy—the Bhismaknagar Fort. The forts of Arunachal Pradesh, though much influenced by the Indian classical tradition, were best suited to the nature of their own terrain and warfare of the day. The four classifications—*vana durga*, or forest fort, the *giri durga*, hill fort, the *ishtika durga*, brick-built fort, and, lastly,

ABOVE AND FACING PAGE
From a self-proclaimed "serial kisser" to a bright red group of *gaon burrahs* donning an assortment of cane hats, the fun quotient is at a high.

The wing of a wrecked Caribou stands at Walong, not far from the War Memorial and the Hut of Remembrance, a silent tribute to the brave souls of 1962.

RIGHT | A young couple from Hawai pose for us.

the *panka durga*, mud fort—can be seen featured together in a single fort in Arunachal. We are told that the Bhismaknagar Palace has been designed as per norms laid out by Kautilya.

The Lohit River enters India at Rima and Kibithu in what is now the Anjaw District. The legends of Parasuram and ancient Indian texts refer to it as the Lauhitya River, originating in the mountains across the border in Tibet, where it is called the Zayul Chu. It runs its turbulent hill course of 190 km (118 mi.) through the Mishmi Hills, with many rivulets flowing into it and earning it the name, River of Blood. This epithet is not entirely due to the lateritic soil colouring its waters but owes its origins to the story of Parasuram, wherein he washed his bloodstained hands in the river after his redemption from the heinous act of beheading his mother. Disgorging into the plains at Brahmakund, it fragments into multiple branches. The waters of the Siang and Dibang Rivers meet the Lohit at Sadiya in Assam and thereafter the Brahmaputra story takes over.

The Tribes and Agriculture of East Arunachal

The Lohit District shares international boundaries with China and Myanmar, which are to the north and east respectively, while the district headquarters are situated at Tezu. The first subcontinental rays of the sun light up the hamlet of Dong, situated in the extreme eastern corner of the region. While the Mishmi people live in the hills, the Tai Khampti, Khamyang, Singpho, Deori and other smaller groups are settled in the plains. The Mishmi festival of Tamaladu, the Khampti and Singpho festival of Sangken and the Parasuram Kund Mela, along with the Brahmaputra Darshan festival, are the highlights of the calendar year. There are also many Buddha *vihar*s, locally called *chong*s, notably at Namsai, Mon-mau and Chowkham.

In this region, among the Mishmi, the Miji are the most recent migrants and are believed to have come from Kachin country. Yet, there is also a belief that the Mishmi are in fact indigenous people. This is borne out by the places of origin recited by the priests during the performance of rituals. The Nim-kwey Cave that stands at the confluence of the Lohit and Tidding Rivers is sacred and central to their religious beliefs, and the priests draw power and inspiration from the cave.

Traditionally, they had trading relations with Tibet and Assam, exchanging musk, medicinal herbs, paper bark and aconite poison for clothing, salt, copperware and swords. Essentially food gatherers and *jhum* cultivators, they often shifted their villages for fresher pastures but are now becoming settled cultivators. The three sub-tribes are further divided into as many as 150 clans and sub-clans and every member shares the responsibility of maintaining the prestige and dignity of his own family group.

The Digaru, or Taraon, are concentrated around Tezu, Hayuliang, Chaglagam and Goiliang in the Lohit and Anjaw Districts. They too are *jhum* cultivators as well as adept craftsmen and weavers. Their settlements are organised by clan and they collectively own the village land. Members of the clan can freely cultivate, hunt, fish, and gather fruit and firewood on village land. They do not name their village but call it by the name of the clan inhabiting it.

The smallest unit of Mishmi society is the *bhui-gung* or *ang-kway*, quite simply "the common house" or "belonging to the same household or family". This comprises a joint family where three generations, the parents, their sons and the grandchildren, live in the same longhouse. The structure is built like a railway wagon with compartments. Well crafted, it can even be three-storeyed and more than 75–100 m (246–300 ft.) long. Each son maintains his own family and a separate hearth within the house. The parents also maintain a separate hearth but are free to dine with whomever they wish. On special occasions—ranging from a good hunt to weddings—common meals, or *gung*s, are enjoyed together.

Even though the Mishmi are patrilineal and patriarchal, like most other tribes, socially, the women are equally placed alongside the men without segregation or seclusion. They join freely in rites and rituals, participating in all ceremonies with wine, song, dance and good-humoured teasing. The Mishmi turn out in all their magnificence during the Tamaladu festival.

In 2004, the sixteenth and then youngest district was carved out of the Lohit District and named Anjaw (since then the state has been further restructured into 25 districts). Its jurisdiction extended over seven administrative units, Hayuliang, Hawai, Manchal, Goiliang, Walong, Kibithu and Chaglagam. After its creation, Anjaw is now the easternmost district of India and its headquarters are located at Hawai, on the banks of the Lohit River at an altitude of 1,296 m (4,251 ft.).

The Mishmi and the Zekhring are the main tribes of this thinly populated region. The rivers, several of them harnessed for

A local Miju Mishmi from Wakro with the ubiquitous *dah* strapped on.

A variety of fruits and vegetables are grown to keep the families self-sufficient. Among them are bananas, oranges and pears, and spices like cardamom, ginger, turmeric. Seasonal plants include yam, tapioca, cucumber, pumpkin, gourd, and the famous chilli.

TOP | The Mishmi grow the poppy plant in small patches in their kitchen gardens to extract the fluid, used for ritualistic purposes.

hydroelectric power projects, are the Krowti, Lam, Dichu, Tidding, Ampani, Dalai, Klung, Lati, Dav, Sarti and Telua. Agriculture predominates and the main crops are paddy, maize, beans and millet, along with apple, orange, plum, pear and cardamom. The trees, depending on the altitude, are pine, *bhola*, *hingori*, hollock, *orima*, *jutuli*, cane and bamboo.

The Lohit region is luxuriantly dotted with poppy fields that have yielded a rich harvest of opium for centuries. The 266 villages of Anjaw and the 222 villages of Lohit District have traditionally cultivated opium for consumption and for use in rituals and medicine. Addiction rates are high, with an estimated 24,000 addicts in the two districts, a figure that has grown considerably over the last couple of decades despite opium being a banned substance. Around mid-March it is extracted from the colourful plants growing anywhere and everywhere, from kitchen gardens to hillsides, in villages and towns. It has brought visible prosperity to the valley, though mostly to the settlements along the all-weather road, which goes right up to the Chinese border at Kahao. Often the land left fallow as part of the *jhum* cycle is used for opium cultivation. Ten thousand hectares are under poppy cultivation and the annual yield is approximately one hundred tonnes. Needless to say this is way beyond the requirement of the registered addicts. The villagers make no secret of the cultivation.

The Supreme Court's orders notwithstanding, more and more forests are being cleared for this "cash" crop and for timber logging. Be it the village of Kondong, Supliang, Tafliang or Raliang, mostly below the poverty line and without healthcare facilities, opium has helped them to survive in more ways than one! It has also brought in that little bit extra, be it rice, or repairs to the flimsy longhouse, a solar panel or a motorcycle.

Previously known as "Meyor", the Zekhring inhabit the Walong and Kibithu circles of the district and have a small population that barely touches the four-figure mark. Originally from Tibet, they fled their homeland in the wake of the floods that devastated the Chimdo region and also to escape persecution by the Tibetan authorities. Migrating into the Lohit Valley at the beginning of the twentieth century they faced fierce opposition from the Mishmi. Unable to withstand the incessant attacks both in the Dri and Mathun Valleys, they extended allegiance to the major clans, paying tributes to their heads. Thereafter, the Imu River was decided upon as the boundary between the two communities.

In the area around Sadiya, the Deori were the priestly class of the Chutiya kings and enjoyed a high status before the ascendancy of the Ahom. They consider themselves to be *jimo-chhayan*, the "children of the sun and the moon". Once the Ahom came to power, they dispersed the Chutiya but permitted the Deori to continue at the shrines of Sadiya. This situation changed drastically when the Khampti ousted the Ahom in the late eighteenth century. They stopped the Deori practice of human sacrifice at the Tamreshwari Temple and killed their head priest, Kendukolai Bor Deori. No longer able to even maintain their temples, the Deori were forced to flee to Choikhowa. Today, they are spread over many parts of Assam, apart from the Lohit and Changlang Districts of Arunachal Pradesh.

Lohit District is also home to the Tai Khampti, a branch of the ancient Tai race. Among the many Tai states that sprang up were the Shan, Thai, Ahom and Khampti. In the mid-eighteenth century, with their kingdom in shambles at the hands of the Burmese king Alomphra, the Tai fled to India across the Patkai Hills through the Chaukang Pass and arrived at the Khomong Plateau. Their first settlements came up on the Tengapani (Te'ng) River, south of Sadiya, with the sanction of the ruling Ahom,

ABOVE | A Deori woman at work at her loom in Choikhowa.

RIGHT | This happy threesome are all smiles at being photographed. Throughout the Northeast it was our delight to show people the photographs we had taken of them, invariably leading to much hilarity. Needless to say, many folks had never been photographed before.

A Tai Khampti dancer performing a story from the popular *Jataka Tales*.

BELOW | The Golden Pagoda at Chowkham, jewel-like and transfixing in its surreal beauty in such a remote part of the country.

with whom they had kinship bonds. In 1794, while the Ahom king Gaurinath Singha was trying to contain the Moamaria Rebellion, the Khampti attacked and ousted the Ahom Sadiya-Khowa Gohain, the Warden of the Marches. Thereafter the Khampti chief arrogated the same title and office to himself. Left with no immediate options, the Ahom had to acknowledge the Khampti Gohain. During the reign of Kamaleshwar Singha, the Khampti pushed even further into the plains, but this time around they were confronted by the Ahom and defeated. The Ahom, however, pardoned the Khampti raja and reinstated him, but once again during the Burmese invasion of Ahom territory, the Khampti once again moved into and occupied the Sadiya region. In 1826, after the Burmese had been defeated, the British took over Tai-Ahom, or Assam. Their aggressive advance into Sadiya in 1839 lead to hostilities which lasted over four years, though, eventually, in the face of the superior firepower of the British, the Khampti were forced to make peace.

Today, this Buddhist tribe, practising the Hinayana or Theravada form of Buddhism, lives in some sixteen villages in the Lohit District and the subdivision of North Lakhimpur. They actually believe in polytheism under the subtle veil of Buddhist pantheism. Every village has a *vihara* called the *kyang* or *bapu-chang*, architecturally styled in the manner of Burmese pagodas. The *bhikku*, or priest, administers to the spiritual needs of the people and guides them in their religious festivities. The Tai-Khampti language is tonal and monosyllabic and is considered to be fairly sing-song in its intonation. The alphabet in its pristine form closely resembles the Northern Shan alphabet of Burma. *Liklai*, their classical literature, boasts thousands of manuscripts that are carefully preserved.

The Vijaynagar Salient lies on a limb, protruding eastwards, surrounded on three sides by Myanmar. It used to take four days to walk along the Nao-Dehing from remote villages to the nearest town of Miao. However, a recent road cut through the Namdapha Tiger Reserve along the east bank of the river has now considerably reduced travel time, though Vijaynagar itself continues to be linked only by air. The Yobin, or Lisu, a small tribe who inhabit this region are a peace-loving agrarian community who have mostly converted to Christianity.

The area of the Nocte, Wancho, Tangsa and Tutsa tribes is spread across the districts of Tirap and Changlang that form the eastern stretch of Arunachal, sharing an international border with Myanmar. Cloaked with prime rainforests, this area became critical to the war effort during World War II with the construction of the Stilwell Road between Ledo in Assam and Kunming in the Yunnan Province of China, crossing into Myanmar via the Pangso Pass. The Jairampur cemetery situated in Changlang is said to contain more graves than any other war cemetery in the Northeast, including Kohima War Cemetery in Nagaland.

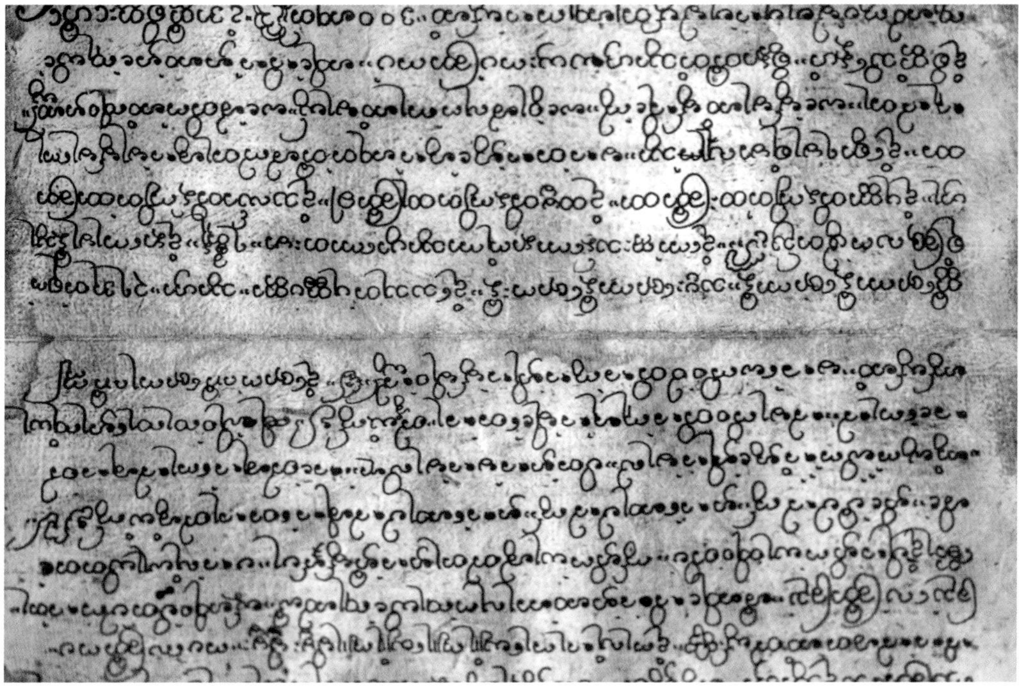

One of the thousands of manuscripts that have been carefully preserved down the generations in monasteries and homes.

Changlang, one of the original 16 administrative districts of Arunachal Pradesh, derives its name from the local word *changlangkan*, which means "hilltop". Interestingly, it is here that the herb used for poisoning fish in the river was discovered. The district is culturally diverse, and boasts of equally distinct flora and fauna. The Namdapha Tiger Reserve is located along the Nao-Dehing River in the rambling tropical rainforest. This is home to the only ape species found within India's boundaries—the hoolock gibbon. It also has the distinction of being the only park in the world to have seven felines, including four of the large cats–namely the tiger, leopard, snow leopard and clouded leopard. Many rivers criss-cross the region, causing frequent flood-like situations and cutting off areas for days together.

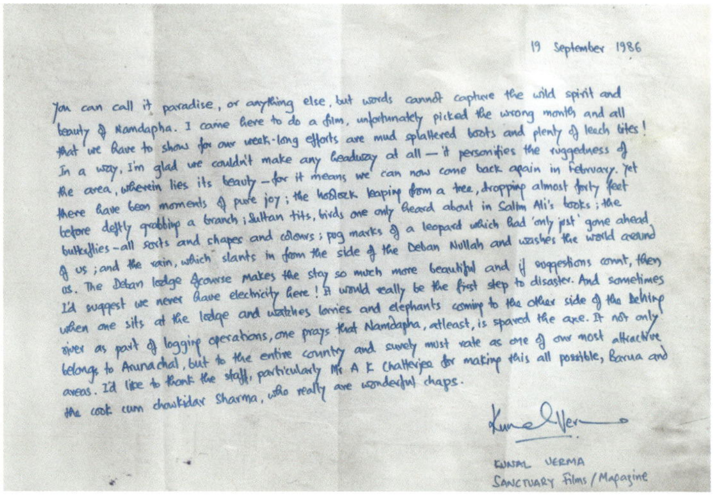

19 September 1986

You can call it paradise, or anything else, but words cannot capture the wild spirit and
beauty of Namdapha. I came here to do a film, unfortunately picked the wrong month and all
that we have to show for our week-long efforts are mud splattered boots and plenty of leech bites!
In a way, I'm glad we couldn't make any headway at all — it personifies the ruggedness of
the area, wherein lies its beauty — for it means we can now come back again in February. Yet
there have been moments of pure joy; the hoolock leaping from a tree, dropping almost forty feet
before deftly grabbing a branch; Sultan tits, birds one only heard about in Salim Ali's books; the
butterflies - all sorts and shapes and colours; pug marks of a leopard which had 'only just' gone ahead
of us; and the rain, which slants in from the side of the Deban Nullah and washes the world around
us. The Deban lodge of course makes the stay so much more beautiful and if suggestions count, then
I'd suggest we never have electricity here! It would really be the first step to disaster. And sometimes
when one sits at the lodge and watches lorries and elephants coming to the other side of the Dehing
river as part of logging operations, one prays that Namdapha, atleast, is spared the axe. It not only
belongs to Arunachal, but to the entire country and surely must rate as one of our most attractive
areas. I'd like to thank the staff, particularly Mr A K Chatterjee for making this all possible, Barua and
the cook cum chowkidar Sharma, who really are wonderful chaps.

Kunal Verma

KUNAL VERMA
SANCTUARY Films / Magazine

The indigenous inhabitants of Changlang District are the Singpho, Tangsa and Tutsa, who are divided into smaller tribes. All the sub-tribes are further divided into a number of exogamous clans. The district is also home to a large number of Chakma tribals who have settled in the forested foothills. Post 1962, a large number of Tibetan refugees made their home in the Choephelling refugee settlement in Miao.

Changlang is also unique for its languages and traditions. Many dialects of the Changlang District are endangered and, with the advent of modernity, some are already extinct. Each tribe has its own traditional religious beliefs and practices. Traditionally, the Tangsa and Tutsa believed in the existence of a supreme being called Rangfrah, and engaged in a shamanistic form of worship. However, in recent years Buddhism and Christianity have influenced many of the people. The Singpho are predominantly Buddhists but the influence of different faiths has led to many of their traditional beliefs becoming incorporated into the practice of Hinayana Buddhism. They are one of the few tribes who are traditional practitioners of permanent settled cultivation. The Singpho rulers had a very cordial relationship with the British Empire during the pre-Independence era, probably as they never ventured to colonise Changlang.

An aerial view of the Deban guesthouse at the Namdapha Tiger Reserve that stands at the entrance to the vast, verdant world of the rainforest.

LEFT | A Singpho trio adding to the colour and cheer of the Namdapha festival, which brings together tribal communities from all the surrounding areas.

FACING PAGE
ABOVE | High up in the endless canopy of trees, the female hoolock gibbon literally holds sway with her darker mate in the forests of Namdapha Tiger Reserve. A few years later, flying overhead in an open-hatch Indian Air Force chopper, we found ourselves mesmerised by the unbroken tree cover, an almost irresistible invitation to float free.

BELOW | Kunal's entry in the visitors' book at the Miao guesthouse, while filming there in 1986. He pointed out that any road built through this section of the Naga Patkai would wreak havoc on the ecology. Years later this would prove to be prophetic.

PREVIOUS PAGES
Nocte women from Khonsa in Tirap District.

A Nocte warrior of Tirap Changlang, a tribe once (in)famous for headhunting.

PRESENT PAGE
Young girls of the Wancho tribe dance, with the *gaon burrah* leading the way, in the village hut, an elaborate affair of bamboo and carvings.

The development of roads and relatively easy access to the communication network of Assam is changing the face of the rural areas within the district, especially around the foothills. On the Namsai-Miao axis, beyond Piyong and Diyum, acre upon acre of previously forested land has been reduced to a sea of tree stumps as more and more land is being brought under tea cultivation. Further south we exit Arunachal Pradesh via Longding District, carved out of the southwestern region of Tirap. The eastern Naga tribes, the Nocte and the Wancho, are ethnically related to the Konyak and bridge the two states as we enter Nagaland.

Nagaland

"Welcome to Khonoma", "Kohima Village Welcomes You", "Welcome to Jakhama"—the famous gateways inviting visitors into each village cheerfully remind them that they are in Naga territory. The villages sit astride hilltops arising from the Brahmaputra plains of Assam and they were originally referred to as Chingmee, or "hill people". Belonging to Indo-Mongoloid stock, some of the distinguishing signs and features of tribal life over millennia have been headhunting, community dances, animal motifs and totems, spiritual healing, as well as the giant log drums, a means of communication between villages. Meeting the Naga people—shaking hands with everyone, especially the *gaon burra*s, drinking rice beer seated in a circle in their huts amidst wood smoke and bamboo—reveals their much celebrated warmth, simplicity, hospitality and ready humour, apart from their tribal formality and reticence. It is also interesting to observe how fluidly the youth move back and forth, from being part of the tribal collective to an urban company complete with Western fashion, music and the latest chic hairstyles. English is the state language but Nagamese, a mix of Assamese, Hindi and Bengali, is the *lingua franca*.

Harvest time is festival time in Nagaland too, just like all over the Northeast, and the Ao of Mukhokchung celebrate the Tsungremmong festival. The village gates are closed to outsiders

Sema women sing in the mist-swathed dawn of Zunheboto as they pound the rice.

and everywhere there is a sea of red, white and black as the people step out in all their traditional finery. Along with the rice beer and food, amusing stories are told by the youth about the elders in the form of folk songs, allowing each individual to flaunt their wit. The Angami of the Kohima Hills have a ten-day celebration of feasting and song, the Sekrenyi festival, which is among the main festivals of Nagaland. Dominated by the drum and flute music that has been passed down the generations, simple and rhythmic dance movements are heightened by the elaborate costumes and spectacular headdresses. The Mongmong festival, celebrated by the Sangtam of Tuensang, heralds the end of months of toil in the fields. This is a time of togetherness and of worship of the god of the house and the three cooking stones. Their hunting festival, Vikhukephru, sees households gather their fishing nets, weapons and other hunting gear and thoroughly cleanse them to ensure plentiful game. The other important festival is Alakakhu, which is marked by every man, old and young, shooting an arrow at a malevolent spirit, thus signifying the chasing away of all epidemics. The Sema of Zuhneboto celebrate the Tuluni festival, raising a cheer to abundance with huge quantities of rice beer, while the Konyak of Mon celebrate Aoleang Monyu at the end of sowing seeds, praying for a bumper harvest. The Chang observe the Naknyu Lum and the Lotha of Wokha observe the Tokhu Emong and Pikhuchak festivals. The Rengma have the Ngada festival, during which one must visit the graves of one's ancestors. The Chakhesang celebrate Tsukhenyie, bringing to an end the post-harvest fun and games, invoking the blessings of the gods and refocusing on the work ahead, and Suhkruhnye, an eleven-day festival during which girls and boys are sanctified. The Zeliang zestfully celebrate the Hega and Ngai Ngai festivals in December, the highlight of which is the dance with men and women holding feathers in their hands.

Like all Naga tribes, the Konyak, too, dance and sing as a community ritual that has remained unchanged through millennia and is very much part of their collective identity.

FACING PAGE

ABOVE | The Angami, who brought great resilience to the fore in their fight to stop the British from overrunning their homeland, proudly welcome you to Khonoma.

BELOW | Peren District near Dimapur, the home of the Zeliang tribe, greets you with a splendid pair of great Indian hornbills, and Zeliang warriors. Entering through these Naga gateways is always an exhilarating experience, creating a buzz of anticipation as yet another part of this magical state reveals itself.

FOLLOWING PAGES

The quintessential image of Nagaland, villages crowning rich green hillsides, with the swirling clouds never very far away. An image to be breathed in with the fresh morning air.

An ever-unfolding canvas of breathtaking beauty, Nagaland is awash with tropical and sub-tropical evergreen forest. Bamboo, rattan and mahogany are the dominant species growing wild in abundance. The rivers that weave through are the Doyang and Diphu to the north, the Barak to the southwest and the Chindwin River flanking the southeastern boundary of the state. Primarily a rural agrarian society, the landscape either has meticulously maintained paddy fields cut into the hillsides or, as is the case with most tribes, the almost shocking barrenness of *jhumming*, the slash and burn cultivation method that over the years has been patented by tribal societies the world over.

Naga villages usually occupy hilltops or the highest possible points along a ridge, largely due to traditional headhunting practices, as inter-village feuds were frequent and being able to dominate the surrounding countryside was critical. The villages are divided into *khel*s, meaning "wards" or "quarters", which are often inhabited by members of a particular clan who claim descent from a common ancestor. At the centre of each *khel* is the *morung*. This is the most prominent house within the village on which the greatest embellishment and care is often lavished, particularly in terms of empanelled wood carvings. In the past, it also served as a guardhouse and was used to stock up all the village's weapons. Often, the *morung* stored the skulls of slain enemies, which were believed to hold their essential fertile powers. And of course the sacred log drum, considered a magical instrument, is traditionally housed here.

Wood carvings, with their signature bold style, continue to be the most striking Naga art form. Using an axe and primitive tools such as the adze and chisel, they carve large or even life-size motifs in high relief on *morung* pillars, crossbeams and front panels of the houses of rich men, the village chief and feast-givers, as well as granary doors and Y-posts. The wood

PRESENT AND FACING PAGE
Some fine representatives of the rich and varied wood carving culture—fierce and lifelike depictions of warriors, the great Indian hornbill, and a vibrant scene from folklore showing the valour of the tribes when faced with nature's fearsome wrath.

used from the local forest includes the Nahor palm wood—the ironwood of the Naga Hills—and the oak. The wood-carvers even now continue to execute a rich variety of carvings while retaining their amazing sense of proportion. Village gates are often carved with motifs symbolising an increase in the local population. The *mithun*, tiger and human heads depict a clan's valour and prowess, meant to instill respect in enemies and protect the clan from them. Stylised patterns of squares with heads were meant to signify successful headhunts. Fallen warriors of the clan are the subject of life-size carvings—an upside down carving, for example, would indicate that the warrior had died bravely in battle and his head had been taken.

Naga life basically has a ritualistic aspect, as the spirits and gods that control the realities of life—disease, human, crop fertility, and rain, among others—need constant appeasing. Most of the animistic beliefs and shamanist practices of the Naga are reflected in their unique artwork, jewellery and costume, as well as in their architecture and craft.

Certain Naga clans identified their communities with certain animals. These species are carved onto totems and are perceived to be either group ancestors or guardian spirits, and clan members identified with the animal's attributes. In northern Naga groups there exist gecko, tiger and frog clans. A curious myth is attached to the great Indian hornbill—every time it is killed it always plummets to the earth head first, which has made it an object of reverence and its feathers are much sought after, leading to the virtual tragic elimination of this majestic bird from this region.

The Colonial History of Nagaland

During the early nineteenth century British dominance in the Assam region was absolute. Tea gardens had sprung up

A proudly displayed gun keeping alive memories of the battles of yore.

BELOW | A painting depicting the arrival of the American Baptist missionary E.W. Clark at the Ao village of Molungkimong, guided by the Assamese interpreter, Godhula Rufus Brown.

FACING PAGE
Soon a Christian brotherhood was formed and Christianity began taking hold. Almost a century and a half later, it dominates the outlook of Naga society, while traditional beliefs and practices try to hold their ground.

everywhere and a clash with the local populace was a matter of time. It became imperative to enforce law and order against the frequent incidents of violence by tribal warriors from the surrounding hillsides, who raided the adjoining tea gardens and murdered British officials, transgressed recognised boundaries, or hunted human heads in the neighbouring villages. Thus, in 1835 the Cachar Levy, the forebear of the Assam Rifles, was raised to guard British interests in the region, extending from the Brahmaputra River to Cachar and to carry out small-scale punitive expeditions in the hill areas. More importantly the British had learnt that the raja of Manipur was planning to incorporate the Naga Hills into his kingdom and so the government in Calcutta decided to bring the Naga tribes under direct British influence instead. To this end E. R. Grange, the civilian officer in charge of Nowgong, was directed to conduct the first expedition into the strongest and most turbulent area, that of the Angami Naga, in 1839.

The internal feuds amongst the Naga, attacks on survey parties, and the murder of several British officers on duty added fuel to the fire and, by 1878, a Forward Policy was in place to gradually extend British authority over all independent tribes. During this process, many British officers lost their lives. In most cases, their heads, weapons and equipment, along with those of their escorts were taken away. Every such expedition generally ended with the British punishing the tribes and annexing their area.

Meanwhile, the year 1872 saw the arrival of the American Baptist missionary, Edward Winter Clark, to the Ao village of Molungkimong. Assisted by his Assamese interpreter, Godhula Rufus Brown, he soon organised a Christian fellowship and baptised those who accepted Christ. In 1894 Mulong became the centre of missions to further the evangelisation of the Naga. Mulong was the first Christian village in Nagaland. A later year, Clark moved his mission centre to Impur, presently known as the Ao Baptist Arogo Mungdang, headquarters of the Baptists. Nagaland is today the most populated Baptist state in the world. Some of Asia's most imposing churches dominate the skyline at Kohima, Dimapur and Mokokchung. Church attendance is high in both rural and urban areas.

Sekrenyi celebrations are in full swing in the hills of Kohima, which are dominated by the Angami.

RIGHT | The Ao youth of Mukokchung honour us with traditional song and dance.

Christianity brought many changes to the traditional animistic world of the Naga. Headhunting was one of the customs frowned upon. Literacy and education were brought in and the schools prescribed the Bible as a textbook. Yet the fabric of village life in its rituals and beliefs, especially festival celebrations, adheres to immemorial practices. Baptists opened several primary and middle schools in the Kohima and Mokokchung areas and a new, educated elite were born out of Christian conversions. Though most of the education in the early 1900s was not secular but religious in nature, Western education has been the binding factor behind Naga nationalism as it broke through the traditional inter-tribal barriers, making way for a sense of oneness.

The Tribes of Nagaland

As we move across Nagaland we get a glimpse into the lives of the resident tribes of the area. Ungma village, straddling a ridge on the outskirts of Mokokchung, is the ancestral and cultural center of the Ao, also known as the Aor, or "those who came", crossing over the hills from the east. The main street of the village proudly displays the tribe's history in the form of statues and plaques that pay homage to their ancestors who were the first settlers. In each village and town, the long log drum is strategically placed with a panoramic view of the hills, facilitating instant communication with the whole community. The story of their origin revolves around the saga of three males and three females arising out of six stones at a place called Lunkgterok. The direct effect of this myth resulted in clan hierarchy and exogamous marriage traditions amongst the Ao. Myths embody the true indigenous nature of the Ao as religious and social customs stemmed from them.

The Ao are perhaps the most outgoing of all Naga tribes. Their specialised products were always sought after and the Ao would periodically come down from the Naga Hills to the bazaars in the plains. The Ao take pride in having schools in every village with Ao teachers, doctors, engineers, scientists and senior administrators and diplomats, as well as a highly evolved social system guaranteeing hereditary rights to tribe members.

Kohima is the capital city of Nagaland and the Angami dominate the hills of Kohima District. They believe in the Khezakenoma legend of origin, which holds that three sons went their separate ways, and became the forefathers of the Angami, Sema and Lotha tribes. Tenyidie is the most commonly spoken language. The Angami are also extremely skilled with their hands—be it woodcraft, bamboo craft, the making of machetes or the weaving of shawls. In fact, there is a methodical neatness about the tribe that is reflected in the layout of their villages and fields as well.

The Angami were one of the few tribes that offered stiff resistance against British intrusion into their territories. In 1831–1833, the British had ordered Manipur to subjugate the Angami. In retaliation the Angami raided the Manipur and North Cachar areas that were under the imperial forces. A century later the British invaded the Angami areas under various pretexts, such

An Ao *gaon burrah* enjoys his cup of cheer.

FOLLOWING PAGES
The battle-ready Sema in full ceremonial regalia.

as Angami intrusion into their territories, the willingness of inhabitants to be under British control, great economic wealth, and social evils like headhunting and slavery, but were once again met with severe retaliation. Clans and villages got together and forced the British to depart from the region and not interfere in Angami internal affairs.

The eastern Angami separated from the rest of the tribe and formed the Chakhesang. Initially, this new tribe was made up of three major sub-tribes, Chokri, Kheza and Sangtam. The name "Chakhesang" came from the first syllable of each group. Later, only the Chokri and Kheza remained, along with a minor group, the Zhamai, or Zhavame, who are settled in Phek District.

The Sangtam, the richest and most colorful of Naga tribes, live in the cold and hilly terrains of Tuensang District, and are believed to have migrated from Myanmar, thus owing their origin to the Burmese-Tibetan race. The term *sangtam* means "those who live in peace". Amongst the tribe the sacred being is understood in relation to land and space. They call their main deity Lijaba. *Li* means "land" and *jaba* means "real", which basically denotes that soil and god are intimately connected. People believe that the supreme being enters into the soil with the seeds and rises again along with the crops. Thus, the blooming flower, and the bearing of fruits and rice, signifies the presence of the Creator. The Sangtam of Tuensang District are a tribe that have embraced Christianity while maintaining the continuity of ancestral beliefs. Their twelve festivals are even today celebrated according to the culture and religion of their ancestors. During the Mongmong festival, observed in the first week of September, the village priest, called *beburu*, solemnly announces, "*Zangnyu mongmong nung eh-lee*," in the dead of the night. Another priest repeats it at daybreak and the preparations begin.

The designs and symbols in the textiles of the Sangtam Naga are very similar to those of the Ao and Yimchunger, while retaining their identifying features. The Sangtam *rongsu* shawl is a warrior shawl that no ordinary person can wear. The aristocracy of the tribe wears a shawl called the *tsingrang su*, the design of which is said to have been revealed to a woman of the Pongen clan in a dream.

In the southern Sangtam country axe-shaped *dao*s held great significance. These prized possessions of the affluent classes, also the preferred weapons for *mithun* sacrifice, were handed down as heirlooms.

Zunheboto District, the heart of Nagaland, is home to one of the great martial tribes of the region, the Sema. Also known as the Sumi tribe, they are the third largest tribe after the Konyak and the Ao and have settled here from time immemorial. They practise both terrace and *jhumming* cultivation and are experts in handicrafts. The Sema have an innate belief in an unseen higher power that shapes destiny. The benevolent Creator, the spirits of the sky, the angels and, finally, the spirits that live among men, have to be propitiated with sacrifices and rituals periodically. The Sema believe in the transmigration of souls. They also believe the head is the receptacle of the soul and of immense vitality and creative energy.

A broad-minded tribe with fascinating customs and traditions, the Sema celebrate Tuluni festival, the highlight of which is the exchange of gift baskets among betrothed couples. Cock-fighting is a popular sport among the Sema youth. It demands superb strength and agility. The contestants rain kicks at eye-baffling speed on each other till one of them surrenders.

The status of women amongst the Sema is considerably high, and marriages are often choice-based for girls. The girl exercises reasonable freedom before marriage and is allowed to move around with her *aluzhili*, or group of friends, which often consists of both sexes. A woman's head with luxurious hair was a highly desired trophy during the headhunting days, as it was assumed to encourage an abundance of crops. Thus in the past, the heads of Sema girls would be shaved till about 12-14 years of age, and only after embarking on the journey of matrimony were they allowed to grow their hair.

A martial tribe renowned and feared for its valour and headhunting practices, the Konyak dominate the Mon District of Nagaland. They are also settled in Myanmar and in the Tirap and Changlang Districts of Arunachal Pradesh, where they are known as Wanchoo Konyak. One of the largest tribes, their villages are known as the lands of their *ang*, or king. Their martial status is also reflected in the death rituals of the Konyak. The dead needed to carry their weapons on their trip to their future home, since each would meet again and fight again all of the warriors they had killed in battle during life.

Social hierarchy amongst the Konyak consists of four distinct classes. The aristocratic class is made up of the *ang*s themselves, followed by the next rung, the descendants of the ang.

Life is good for the ang, or king, of the Konyak village of Mon.

FACING PAGE
A much-awaited sporting festival has the Sema women participating in full strength.

The *morung* retells many stories through carvings.

Commoners who have proved meritorious in various fields are slotted into the third tier, while the last class consists of simple village people. The *ang*, being the king, is considered sacred and his word, the law. Before the advent of Christianity, the Konyak were one of the few tribes that believed in the existence of one supreme deity—Gawang, which literally means "earth-sky".

The Chang tribe of Tuensang believe in the oneness of nature, man and supernatural forces. During Naknyu Lum, their most important festival, each household lights a central fire. On this occasion, the footpaths and all the houses are decorated with a herbal shrub called *ngounaam* (*Elsholtzia blanda* or Himalayan mint), which is planted in front of every house to ward off evil spirits.

The traditional home of the Lotha tribe is the Wokha District. The Lotha and the Rengma were believed to be the same tribe until there arose a conflict between the Rengma villages and the Lotha village of Phiro. A tribe of headhunters, the Lotha gave up the practice when they converted, en masse, to Christianity.

The villages vibrate with song and dance when the festivals of Tokhu Emong and Pikhuchak are celebrated. The social status of the men is clearly distinguished by the shawls they wear. The prestigious shawl for men is the *lungpensu* that they are entitled to wear after offering several feasts to the community and completing the ritual dragging of a stone. The prized shawl for women is the *opvuram* shawl.

The Zeliang, residing near the Manipur border, are a sub-tribe of the Kachha Naga that migrated to mainland Nagaland in the eighteenth century. The name originates from two words *ze* and *liang*, after the two communities Zemei, or Zemi, and Liangmei, which united to form the Zeliang tribe. The tribe was opposed to British authority and rebelled against the Empire in 1933 as part of a secessionist movement. This indigenous population is humble and unsophisticated and some of them hold on to their animistic traditional beliefs, though they are a minority in a Christian-dominated population. They are generally monogamous and practise the custom of bride price, which consists of *mithun*, ornaments, land and money. Divorce

ABOVE | The village nerve centre, the *morung* is known by different names by the different tribes. *Haku* for the Chang, *singtan* in Sangtam, *kichuki* among the Angami, *arju* for the Ao, *chumpo* in Lotha, *apuki* in Sema, and so on.

LEFT | A senior Chang warrior, who displays his headhunting prowess even today.

The Dimapur monoliths display many themes from nature as part of the religious and social iconography.

FACING PAGE
A Zeliang youth wearing the tribe's distinctive headgear. The popular folksongs and folktales of this tribe range in subject from migration to agriculture, and from headhunting to songs about the self.

FOLLOWING PAGES
Chang men in full headhunting attire, which includes a little basket attached to the back to bring back the heads in!

is allowed but a woman has to return the bride price. Zeliang women are known for their beauty and expertise at handlooms, while the men are proficient in crafting bamboo and cane handicrafts.

Dimapur, situated in the plains, is the commercial hub of Nagaland. It was the capital of the Kachari dynasty that ruled the region in the thirteenth century. The ruins from this period are scattered in and around the town, giving a glimpse of the magnificence of this now forgotten kingdom. The monoliths are indicative of a megalithic culture that was non-Aryan and yet was somewhat influenced by Hinduism.

Nagaland since Independence

Nagaland was the scene of the Battle of Kohima in 1944, during World War II, which turned the tide of the Japanese offensive into India. Famously known as the Battle of the Tennis Court, Earl Louis Mountbatten sums up its significance as "probably one of the greatest battles in history... in effect the Battle of Burma... naked unparalleled heroism." The Kohima War Cemetery lies on the slopes of Garrison Hill in what was the actual scene of the battle. British and Indian forces lost around 4,000 men, dead, missing or wounded. The Japanese lost more than 5,000, halting their advance into India.

The period leading to Independence saw the process of socio-political mobilisation gain momentum. In the early 1950s, Zapu Phizo, an Angami, voiced the claim that the Naga Hills and Tuensang District had never been part of British India and hence, he was fighting for the sovereignty of Nagaland as a separate nation. It was around him that the radical elements of the Naga National Council gravitated. A strong sense of Naga identity emerged to forge solidarity across traditional tribal divides. Among the tribal elite that was then at the helm, not many were sympathetic to the underground movement and instead focused on building the state of Nagaland. In the wake of this, for instance, many Chakhesang who lived elsewhere returned to their homeland.

In 1963, while proclaiming Nagaland as India's sixteenth state, the then Prime Minister Jawaharlal Nehru spoke of their distinctive way of life that should find expression to the fullest

ABOVE | Uneasy lies the peace between mainstream India and Naga insurgents, as this stone indicates.

BELOW | Questions about hunting birds and animals are simply shrugged off by the locals. These civets were strung up for sale on the road to Kohima.

FACING PAGE
The memorial to the Battle of Kohima silently overlooks the suburban spread.

in the new state. Verrier Elwin observed how the Naga were "today awake and stirring, anxious to progress. They are a fine people of whom their country is proud, strong and self-reliant, with a free and independent outlook characteristic of highlanders everywhere." Nagaland has seen a prolonged period of insurgency and negotiations over the decades while the evolving democratic process places the state in the mainstream of India's politics today.

Political issues apart, the Naga tribes today face severe ecological problems as well. It is ironic that the land of the hornbill is virtually devoid of the majestic flying creatures. Nagaland actually has the dubious distinction of having "silent forests" where, though the primary jungle has been replaced by other vegetation, there is an eerie silence as most creatures, big and small, have long ago been hunted and killed. The key issue in the Naga Patkai is water, as most Naga villages continue to cling to defendable hilltops. Earlier, the practice of shifting cultivation (*jhumming*) and the excessive killing of animals and birds was absorbed by nature, but with better roads leading to better accessibility, the toll on the land is beginning to tell. Some tribes like the Chakhesang developed a unique system of rainwater harvesting called *zabo* long ago. This required the impounding of water. It consisted of a protected forestland at the summit of a hill, water-harvesting tanks in the middle and cattle yard and paddy fields at the lower side. The system enhanced crop productivity and facilitated water resource management by checking deforestation through various cultural rituals. Many of these time-honoured practices are dying out today. More than ever, deforestation, alongside the traditional burning of forests, needs to be totally prohibited to check the environmental denudation of a fantasy land.

Manipur

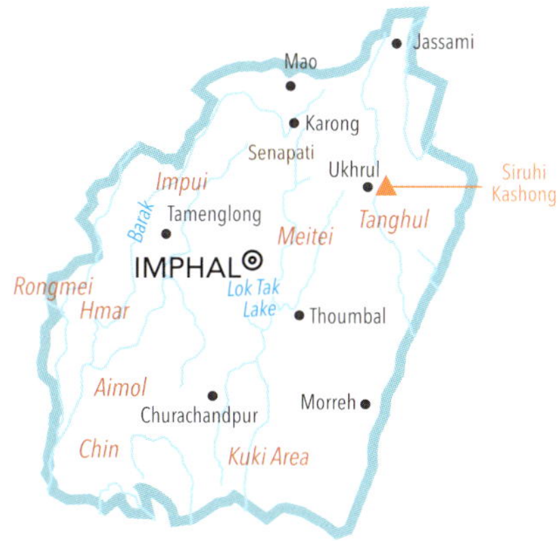

Moirang, at a short distance from Imphal, the capital of Manipur, had its moment at the height of the freedom movement and the Japanese onslaught during World War II. It was here that the Tricolour of India was hoisted for the first time on Indian soil, by Colonel Malik of the Azad Hind Fauj (INA), on April 14, 1944. The headquarters of the INA, then located in Moirang, survive today as a motor mechanic's garage. A museum nearby carries some of the memorabilia of that time of "Unity, Faith and Sacrifice", as the credo reads. Needless to say, not many know of Moirang and its historic importance. In 2009, the authors met two former INA soldiers—a Kuki nursing assistant, Thongkhonga M. Haokip, and a Tangkhul Naga, Lieutenant Ringshi Keishing, both of whom were living witnesses to the Battle of Sangshak, fought in 1944. They were part of a large number of local people who joined Subhash Chandra Bose's army.

Manipur has a central bowl-shaped valley surrounded by steeply rising hills of the Burrail and Manipur Hill Ranges. Landlocked and almost like a fortress, Manipur finds itself enclosed by the Naga Hills to the north, Myanmar to the east, the Lushai and Chin Hills to the south and the state of Assam on its southwestern flank. Of the two river systems that drain Manipur, the Barak River and the Manipur River, the latter flows through the Imphal Valley. A prevalent myth of origin relates

The floating marvels of Loktak Lake—its globally unique ecosystem of *phumdi*, a heterogeneous mass of vegetation, soil and organic matter.

Lieutenant Ringshi Keishing, a Tangkhul Naga veteran of the INA, lives to tell the story.

TOP | Netaji Subhash Chandra Bose pausing to study a map during the onward push of the Azad Hind Fauj.

that Manipur was land reclaimed from water by Lord Shiva's *trishul*, or trident. Another myth makes it the place illuminated by the crown jewel of the Shesh Nag for the *raaslila* of Lord Shiva and Parvati after sunset. Mythological references from the *Mahabharata* suggest that Arjuna and Chitrangada met here in Manipur. The state was then known as Monglei, and the *Mahabharata* and the *Skanda Purana* refer to it as Mekhele, while others called it Cassay.

The History of Manipur

An independent kingdom with a 2000-year-old history, Manipur was the last princely state to come under British colonial rule. Its first recorded kingdom was established in the year 33 CE, with the coronation of King Pakhangba. Formed by the unification of ten major tribes, the present-day population of Manipur can be seen as two major ethnic groups—the Meitei, who are the majority and inhabit the valley, and the Naga, together with the Kuki, who are the people of the hills. After Pamheiba Raja made Hinduism the official religion of Manipur, his grandson, Maharaja Bhagyachandra (1759–1798), decided to go a step further, spreading Vaishnavism and creating a unified Manipur. He is also famous for being the creator of the Ras Leela, a form of classical Manipuri dance depicting the love story of Krishna and Radha. The *Chaitharol Kumbaba* (*Royal Chronicles*) records the chronology of the royal family of Manipur.

The transformation of the Meitei from believers in the indigenous Sanamahi religion into a predominant Hindu kingdom, wherein an essentially tribal people converted their society completely, has had a deep socio-political impact on the entire region. Although Hinduism impacted Manipur only during King Charairongba's (King Pamheiba's father) reign, in the beginning of the eighteenth century, it evolved as the dominant religion in the Imphal Valley thereafter. Along with the rulers of Assam, the Manipuri kings played a major role in the emergence of Hinduism as a major force in the Northeast.

What followed was the destruction of all religious records pertaining to the Sanamahi religion. There was a ban on the Meitei Meyak—the ancient Manipuri script—and the singing of traditional songs, while all residual aspects—social, cultural or related to rituals and customs—were abolished. But the old gods were not completely forgotten. The Manipuri retained aspects of the original ancient animistic religion, rich in myth and ritual. Devotion to their supreme god Lainingthou Soralei and following

PRESENT AND FOLLOWING PAGES
The Imphal Valley is the rice bowl of Manipur. Never-ending rice fields stretch in all directions.

in his footprint is an accepted practice today. Every Manipuri Hindu home has a Sanamahi Kaachin, which is the southwestern corner where a lamp is kept burning. Many festivals, like the Lai-Haraoba, dedicated to the traditional gods and goddesses are kept alive with the same fervour of ancient times, even though some of the dance forms have gone through their own evolutionary cycle as they moved from a pagan to a more Hindu form like the Ras Leela.

Conferred the title of "Vidyaratna", Pandit Atombapu Sarma (1889–1963), the chief priest of Manipur and a reputed scholar, played a significant role in knitting together the historical, ancient world of the Meitei with the Brahmanical traditions that have become a patented brand of Manipuri Hinduism—an epitome of rich social and cultural traditions.

Unlike most other peoples of the Northeast whose society evolved in comparative isolation, Manipur was in constant touch with other communities—ranging from the Thai to the Chinese to the Burmese kingdoms. The Manipur ruling class presided over a kingdom that was constantly in a state of flux. By the mid-1760s, Manipuri royals were in touch with the British in Chittagong, seeking their help to further their own ends including fighting the Burmese.

During the early nineteenth century, internal crises, along with the seven-year devastation wrecked by the Burmese War, gave the British a chance to get a foothold in the state. With Prince Gambhir Singh allied on their side, the British succeeded in defeating the Burmese. The situation in Manipur then stabilized and Gambhir Singh became the titular king, although effective powers passed into the hands of the British and their interference continued to grow during the reign of Maharaja Surchandra Singh. His general, Senapati Tikendrajit, himself a prince, was increasingly apprehensive of the British, given their unstated objective of seizing Manipur and making it a colony.

What followed was the Palace Revolt on September 22, 1890, led by Tikendrajit and other princes. The king fled and Tikendrajit established the king's brother, Kullachandra, in his place with himself as the heir apparent. The ousted ruler petitioned the British for help. The chief commissioner of Assam, J.W. Quinton, was sent in with the sole objective of apprehending Tikendrajit. On the evening of March 24, 1891, when the men, women and children were watching a Ras Leela performance, a 600-strong British force attacked the palace compound, taking many innocent lives. The people retaliated and six British officers were killed while the routed soldiers fled. Later, the British retaliated in full force and members of the royal family were arrested, and Bir Tikendrajit and Lungthoubu Thangal, popularly known as the Thangal General, who was his brother-in-arms, were hanged before the public after a farcical trial amid a storm of public protest. Queen Victoria's appeal for amnesty was also ignored. August 13, remembered as Patriots' Day in Manipur, is the martyrdom day of this "Lion of Manipur".

The politicisation of Manipur, as we know it today, started in 1934 when the Nikhil Hindu Manipuri Mahasabha was formed under the patronage of the then Manipur king. World War II further reinforced political consciousness among the Manipuri elite. From the Indian perspective it was least expected that, with their Vaishnavite faith, some sections of Manipuris would resist integration with the Indian mainland. A pan-Mongolian movement started in Manipur in 1956–57, that laid the foundation for insurgency and gave decisive impetus to the agitation for statehood. Revival of "cultural hegemony" of history was started by young Meiteis, harking back to their Mongoloid, pre-Hindu Sanamahi past, demanding that the old name for Manipur, Kangleipak, as well as the old script and the traditional calendar be adopted.

For many Vaishnavas of Imphal the day begins with offering prayers at the Shree Govindajee Temple.

FACING PAGE
A Meitei pundit.

A vigorous physical culture finds expression in traditional martial arts as well as in today's popular sports of bodybuilding, weightlifting, rowing and boxing, among others.

In the complex web of politics that exists in the Northeast, insurgency in Manipur began as an ideological movement for the restoration of the pre-British supremacy of the Meitei. However, owing to the emergence of multiple power centres with their own agendas, the movement turned into an ethnic conflict; the growth of Naga militancy, combined with the fact that it was closely linked to the Nagas of Manipur, made the insurgent movement more of a power struggle. A certain segment of Meitei youth who followed Arambam Somorendra Singh, formed the United National Liberation Front (UNLF) under his leadership and launched an underground movement. Over the years insurgency in Manipur has evolved into a hydra-headed monster, with the common citizen more often than not being caught in the crossfire between the multiple underground organisations and the security forces.

Manipuri Culture

The inherent artistic nature of the people, along with deeply embedded traditions, has found expression in distinctive classical, folk and martial dances. They say it is difficult to find a Manipuri girl who does not sing or dance. Manipuri dance spells the magic of the Ras Leela with gestures and movements that have enthralled people for centuries. Nupa Pala, or the Kartal Cholom, is a group performance by male dancers, dressed in white, singing and dancing to the accompaniment of the *mridanga* and cymbals. Starting slowly, the dance keeps gathering momentum until it climaxes in a blur of movement. The Pung Cholom, or Manipuri *mridanga* dance, is performed as an invocation before the Sankirtana and the Ras Leela. Once again, the dance spirals from a soft whisper to a thunderous climax. The Lai-Haraoba, an annual ritual festival of the Meitei, showcases the Maibi dance in which the priestesses trace the whole cosmogony of the Meitei way of life.

The martial arts of Manipur have evolved as the Thang-Ta, or sword-spear dances. Traditional items like Takhousaba, Thang-Chungoi Yannaba and others showcase combatants with swords, spears and daggers in solo, duet and group ensembles. Three major festivals—Kwaktalba (Dussera), Lai-Haraoba (the rejoicing of the gods) and the Chiranba—are celebrated with accompanying song and dance by both sexes. In the past, experts of Thang-Ta were maintained in the royal courts because the dance form not only provides basic training in warfare, but also develops physical and mental strength and agility. Symbolically, it is believed that the movement of the *thang*, or sword, wards off evil spirits, while the *ta*, or spear, is held in a protective position.

The *cholom*s fall under the *tandav* category of dances, belonging to the Chalanam group. Dhol Cholom, meaning "beating of drums", marks the celebration of the Holi festival. This dance is restricted to male performers, who string the *dhol* around their shoulders and beat it in unison. This is accompanied by acrobatic twirls, as they leap around in joyful abandon in a particular rhythmic pattern, manifesting the ambiance of the festival. The dancers wear customary men's attire like the *dhoti*, with or without a *kurta*, and a stole-like cloth. The performance requires immense stamina owing to the vigour of the movements and

LEFT | The legendary beauty of Manipuri women is best seen in the bejeweled splendour of a bride about to take her marriage vows.

RIGHT | The Ras Leela, which has mesmerised people through millennia, holds the audience in rapt attention.

beating of drums. Like many other dance forms from Manipur, this dance draws its inspiration from martial arts but without the incorporation of any weapons, and its steps are inspired by nature. Dhol Cholom has gathered much popularity in recent years and many classical dance institutes have incorporated it into their curriculum.

The wedding ceremony of the Meitei, called *luhongba*, is a very elaborate affair. It is compulsory for the bride to wear the Ras Leela skirt, accompanied by ornate headgear, called *kajenglei*, as she is seen as an epitome of the *gopis*. The men dress in a *dhoti* and *kurta*, while women adorn themselves in a pink sari-like *phanek* and a white *chadar* for the occasion. Women's high status among the Meitei is reflected in the non-observance of the *ghungat* by the bride during the wedding. Even after marriage she retains her *sagei*, or sub-clan identity, despite surrendering jural rights to her parental home. There is another form of marriage practiced among the Meitei called the *chenba*, or marriage through elopement. Here, a girl and boy leave their parents' house without the consent of the elders. The next morning a few elderly people from the boy's family report to the girl's house. They seek forgiveness for their son's behavior, and request their counterpart to arrange a wedding. If the girl's father consents, only then the *luhongba* is organized.

The city of Imphal boasts of the Ima Keithel, the Ima Market or Khwairamband Bazaar, the only market in the world run exclusively by women, or *imas* (mothers). In the past, it was

The *sangai* or the *thamin*, the brow-antlered deer.

FACING PAGE
The serenity of Loktak Lake, which has inspired Manipuri poets since time immemorial.

FOLLOWING PAGES
Rice transplanting in progress at Ukhrul, the home of the Tangkhul Naga of Manipur.

the responsibility of Meitei males to serve the king for the development of the state, and therefore it was the women who became active on the economic front. Ima Market is assumed to have been established by King Khagemba in 1580, and is divided into various segments like New Market, Purana Bazaar and Lakshmi Bazaar. Each division specialises in specific sales: household objects, pottery and fabric, vegetables, fruits and other grocery items, and silver. Around 3,000 women gather here everyday, from the wee hours of the morning till seven in the evening. The women mostly belong to the hill districts of Senapati, Bishnupur, Ukhrul, and Churachandpur. No man is allowed to establish a shop here. The market is reflective of the independent spirit and enterprising nature of Manipuri women.

The Sangai, or Brow-Antlered Deer

Loktak Lake, located near Moirang, is the largest freshwater lake in northeastern India with its unique ecosystem. It is perhaps the only one of its kind globally, where a heterogeneous mass of vegetation, soil, and organic matter, locally called *phumdi*, floats on the surface of the lake. This floating mass is home to the *sangai*, the highly endangered Manipuri brow-antlered deer.

The largest single mass of *phumdi*, which constitutes the Keibul Lamjao National Park, is in the southeastern part of the lake, covering an area of 40 sq km (15 sq. mi.). *Phumdi* are solid enough here to have huts built on them, mainly constructed by local fishermen. Many of the huts have been converted into permanent dwellings and about 4,000 people live in these floating residences, and the art of living on the lake is called *phumshang*. The huts are constructed using plastic ropes, heavy rocks, wood, bamboo, zinc plates, iron rods and other material which blocks penetration of sunlight into the lower depths of the water body.

Gangte youngsters gather around an old couple in the village of Santing near Aina.

There is a saying in Manipur, "*Loktak eepak samudra konggo, Loktakna manipurgi khoidouni*", which means, literally, that Loktak is very big to the people of Manipur but just like a bubble in comparison with the sea. The beauty of the lake has inspired Meitei poets since time immemorial. It is considered the navel of Manipur due to its socio-economic and cultural significance. The staple diet of the state is directly linked to the Loktak as extensive fishing is carried out here. It has traditionally been an open capture fishery. To the present day, Loktak accounts for sixty per cent of total fish production in the state.

The *sangai*, also known as the *thamin*, is imbedded deep in the legends and folklore of the Manipuris. According to a popular folk legend, the *sangai* binds the soul between humans and nature. The slaying of a *sangai*, an unpardonable sin, is hence conceived as the snapping of the umbilical cord between humans and nature. Identified as one of the extremely rare animal species in the entire world, the *sangai* is synonymous with the Imphal Valley. First discovered in Manipur in 1839 and named *Rucervus eldii eldii*, it was subsequently reported as an extinct species by 1951. One of India's greatest environmentalists and photographers, E.P. Gee, rediscovered the animal, which he fondly called "the dancing deer", describing the way they delicately step on uncertain terrain.

The Hill Districts of Manipur

Out of the total of nine districts in Manipur, five are located in the hills and cover an area of 20,089 sq km (7,756 sq. mi.), while the valley covers merely 2,238 sq km (864 sq. mi.). Senapati, Tamenglong, Churachandpur, Chandel and Ukhrul are together grouped as hill districts. Rice farming is practiced in the area through a system of *jhum* cultivation. About seventy per cent of the land is under forest cover and approximately 500 varieties of orchids are found in the region. The hill districts have been facing racial tension since the early 1990s. The Kuki and the

Churachandpur is home to the Chin, Kuki, Mizo and Zomi tribes, who are also found across the borders in Myanmar and Bangladesh.

BELOW | The life of tribal villages throbs with the gaiety of the tiny members of the populace.

An Impui village resounds with song and dance.

RIGHT | Among the total of about forty Naga tribes, half of them make their home in Manipur alone.

Naga have been at each other's throats, giving rise to questions of ethnic interest and ethnic identity. There is further conflict arising from the fact that most development work is carried out in the valleys and the hill districts remain marginalised. Religious discrimination also plays a role as the Meitei are Hindus and most of the tribal sections follow Christianity.

Also adding to the ferment, the All Naga Students' Association of Manipur (ANSAM), supported by United Naga Council (UNC), have constantly reinstated their assertion that the four hill districts of Manipur, apart from Churachandpur, are but a part of the Greater Nagalim Movement. The iridescent Tangkhul tribe resides mostly in the Ukhrul District, which was marked out first as a sub-division in 1919 during the British Raj. A leading tribe in the hills of Manipur as also in parts of Nagaland, the Tangkhul were among the earliest to receive Christianity and are westernised in their culture and education. They have a different language and customs from the other Naga tribes. Locally known as "Hao", this indigenous population is very industrious, and the Tangkhul dominate in various aspects of Naga political and social life. There is a fair amount of jostling for power and position between them and the other Nagas like the Angami and the Ao. Efforts to bring them together have not been successful.

The Tangkhul follow an egalitarian approach in their interpersonal relationships, and therefore it is not surprising to find that a Tangkhul woman has as much independence in her field of activity as her male counterparts. Pettigrew College was established in 1896, and Ukhrul became the first tribal area to get a school in Manipur. Education spread fast among the Tangkhul, and women also reaped its benefits. These women are some of the most educated in Manipur, and many of them have excelled in prestigious arenas like the civil services and academics. The brilliance of Tangkhul women is not surprising, as even during the headhunting days, women used to act as mediators and intervene in the face of a crisis.

Out of the five hill districts of Manipur, Senapati is the smallest in area but has the largest population. It is home to four Naga tribes: Mao, Maram, Thangal and Poumai. Among these four tribes, the Mao are not only the greatest in number but also

Manipuri polo at all times is a crowd-pleaser with its raw energy and sheer speed of action.

the most powerful. Traditionally, the clan and the chief held major power over the social system but with the adoption of Christianity and elimination of animism this power has passed onto the hands of the Church. However, there are reminiscences of a rich cultural heritage in their weaving patterns, which often portray intricate symbols. The art of weaving is carried out exclusively by women, and is considered a taboo for men. *Katesa* is the most common and the oldest of the traditional shawls and *mekhala*s of the Mao women. It is either worn casually or formally on festive occasions in a variety of colours except red, which is reserved for men.

A hundred kilometres (62 mi.) southeast of Imphal, in Chandel District, lies the border town of Moreh. It has become commercially important ever since Indo-Myanmar border trade was opened for 22 items. Ten thousand people cross the international border every day to shop for mostly low-priced Chinese and Thai goods at Namphalong, situated just opposite Moreh in Myanmar. Primarily an ethnic Kuki town, it also houses several other groups, including Manipuri Meitei, Muslims, Tamils, Nepalese and Punjabis, and the annual trade turnover is estimated to be more than ₹1,600 crore ($224,000,000 USD).

Manipuri Polo

The story of the Imphal Valley would be incomplete without a look at Manipuri polo. Sagol-kangjei is the local name for Manipuri polo, *sagol* for "horse" and *kangjei* for the bamboo mallet. A fast paced "must-see" game that would convert even the most world-weary, Manipuri polo has very ancient origins—it can be traced back to 3100 BCE. According to myth, the Umang Lais, or tree gods, lead by Marjing, Thangjing, Wangbrel and Khoriphaba, among others, played the game at the beginning and thereafter passed it down to the people from generation to generation.

From the time of the first Meitei king, Nongda Lairen Pakhangba (Jabista), who, according to myth, ruled Manipur from 33 CE to 153 CE from Kangla, the divine game became the

Dhol Cholom is a popular subject for Manipuri artists, the fluid lines bringing alive the jaw-dropping movements.

FACING PAGE
Endless rows of fresh fruits and vegetables at Imphal's Ima Market.

showpiece event of all major state functions and festivals. It was traditionally played at coronations and became integral to festivities like the Lai Haraoba.

Under active royal patronage the game evolved, and by the time King Khagemba took the reins to the kingdom in the late sixteenth century, Manipuri polo had become a keenly contested military sport. The *pana*-wise system of playing emerged—each *pana* being an administrative unit. Khagemba's victory over the Chinese and, later, Maharaja Pamheiba's overwhelming success against the Burmese was mainly due to the flair and skill of the Manipuri cavalry—all very skilled at both polo and *arambai*, the art of throwing poisoned darts from horseback.

In the mid-nineteenth century a group of British officers and tea planters were fascinated by the game. They learnt to play it from Maharaja Chandra Kirti Singh's militia, who were at the time stationed in Cachar. Thereafter, a modified version of the game was introduced as "English polo", the indigenous Manipuri polo being considered too vigorous, wild and risky. In 1859 this version became the international style of polo and over time reached the far corners of the world, though it continues to be perceived as a royal game. Manipuri polo continues to be played in a warlike fashion, the game being open to all sorts of vigorous, untamed play, not bogged down by too many rules. Players are free to make any moves, however dangerous, to secure victory for their side. During the days of royal patronage, the team wearing red represented the king and was selected from the Ahallup and Laipham *pana*s, while the team representing the queen in yellow was selected from the Khabam and Naharup *pana*s. Though the days of royal patronage are over, the people are even today proud inheritors of the game evolved by their ancestors.

WARNING

Meghalaya

The "Abode of Clouds", that is Meghalaya all year round. Rain fringes, surrounds, is underfoot, clings to and defines almost everything. Undulating highlands oft swathed in mist are what have given Meghalaya the alias "Scotland of the East". Meghalaya is the wettest state in India, with an average rainfall of over 1,200 cm (39 ft.) annually. There are only two seasons per year—the monsoons and the winter!

Meghalaya was once a coral island rising from a tropical ocean. The land rose and fell many times, accumulating several layers of limestone in the downthrusts and building up sandstone deposits in the upthrusts. Entire mangrove forests were buried and doomed to become coal. These sedimentary rocks, with a depth potential of 550 m (1,803 ft.), plus a high elevation and the world's highest precipitation, presented ideal conditions for the formation of caves. Subterranean passages dart in and out of the hillsides, with many of these worlds yet to be discovered. Speleologists, scientists and enthusiasts have recently recorded a thousand caves strung along a 300 kilometre (186 mi.) belt across the southern and southeastern borders of the Mikir, Khasi, Jaintia and Garo Hills. Only about 520 of them, with a combined length of 280 km (174 mi.), have been explored and mapped, disproving

A centuries-old practice among the Khasi and Jaintia tribes, seen in the southern part of the state, is crafting bridges out of living aerial roots of rubber fig trees (*Ficus elastica*), each more spectacular than the last. These root bridges are strong and remain healthy as long the plant becomes stronger over time, as it often in fact does.

the bored myth that there is nothing remaining to discover in the world! There is a famous cave at Syndai, known as the "Brahmine Cave of Sylhet", which is known to be the place of refuge where the Jaintia rajas secured their families during times of war.

Meghalaya includes the Khasi, Garo, Jaintia and Assam Ranges within its borders. It represents the detached extension of peninsular India towards the northeast. Part of this region lies buried under the alluvium deposited by the extensive Ganga-Brahmaputra system of rivers. The Meghalaya Plateau (also called the Shillong Plateau) of the Garo-Khasi Ranges is joined to the Himalayan system at its eastern extremity by the Patkai Range and, in the south, to the Arakan Yoma of Myanmar by the hills of Manipur. The lower portion of these hills is forest-clad, while the upper and central reaches are characterised by undulating hills. The rock formations are among the oldest in the region.

Meghalaya's topography sustains its rich natural vegetation, ranging from the tropical mixed forests of the Garo Hills to the high-altitude pine forests around the Shillong Peak. Coal mining and unregulated felling have totally destroyed large forested sections in this region, though, fortunately, some inaccessible areas remain unaffected. The subtropical forests abound in diverse flora and fauna. The wildlife includes the tiger, leopard, black bear, the Indian *gaur* or bison, and the *sambar*. The Garo Hills in particular, extending up to Baghmara, have retained a healthy population of elephants.

The Tribes of Meghalaya

Meghalaya was under the parallel rule of the Khasi, Garo and Jaintia tribes before the British entered the region. The Khasi are said to be immigrant tribes who arrived from Myanmar and first settled in the plains of eastern Assam. Later, having made Meghalaya Hills their home, the Khasi ruled independently until they became an integral part of the British Empire in 1765. The Garo, on the other hand, trace their origins to Tibet, from where they migrated to what is today Cooch Behar and then onto Dhubri and finally to the Habraghat Pargana neighbourhood, where the earliest Garo kingdom was established, its first ruling prince being Abrasen. After further wanderings, the Garo people moved into the hills. With the coming of the British, all the semi-independent estates that bordered the Garo Hills were brought under their control but the area was formally annexed only in 1873.

A Khasi couple of the Cherrapunji area.

FACING PAGE
Floral riches and quiet streams of the unspoilt virgin forests have been revered and protected by the Khasi and Jaintia alike as the Law Lyngdoh, or Sacred Grove, since time immemorial. The pitcher plant (*Nepenthes khasiana*), above right, is a noteworthy denizen, being a carnivorous plant that is perfectly capable of photosynthesising food but prefers to snap up insects, bacteria, snakes and toads instead.

The Jaintia tribes, who share a megalithic culture with the Khasi, once had their own kingdom with an illustrious history. The Jaintia kingdom, whose origin is unknown, comprised villages that were located in a particular region under a single political unit. They were annexed by the British East India Company in 1835, as part of the Raj's effort to bring all the tribes under one common administrative unit. The Hajong and Banai Koch are other tribes settled in Meghalaya.

Of the seven districts that make up Meghalaya, East Khasi remains the most populated, with the city of Shillong as its district headquarters. The Khasi and the Jaintia call themselves "Ki Hynniew Trep", which means "people of the seven huts". Mentioned in the *Bhagwat Purana*—an Indo-Aryan work—the people belong to the Proto-Australoid Mon-Khmer race, with a light yellow to brown complexion, aquiline nose and a high nasal bridge, some of the earliest ethnic groups of settlers from Burma.

There are four main territorial groups among the Khasi, and the tribe comprises various clans that trace their descent from *kiaws*, or ancestresses. Ancestor worship is of paramount importance to the Khasi, and Ka Lawbei, the tribal Mother, is the most revered. The Khasi are a matrilineal as well as patriarchal society. Lineage is traced through the mother and children take her family name. The father's clan is respected for having given life but his family name is not recognised. The eldest brother exercises authority in important family matters while the youngest daughter is the keeper of the faith and also owns the largest share of the family property. Though society is egalitarian, only certain families are eligible to send a male member for the office of *syiem*, or chief, in the Khasi *hima*, or state. The priests are always from the Lyngdoh clan.

There has been a sea change in social norms, especially among the Christian and urbanised Khasi. Westernisation has led many to move away from the matrilineal model. Education has been the prime mover that has widened the field from the traditional market economy, based on agriculture, to white-collar professions for men and women alike. College professors, engineers, doctors and many other professionals abound. The Khasi have responded well to development programs, whether these are governmental, missionary or social.

Despite the changing face of society, the Khasi religion continues to flourish. The Creator is a masculine god, U Blei Nogthaw,

ABOVE | The draw of the big city, Shillong. The capital city continues to grow in its vast spread, with expanding educational facilities, the Shillong Lajong FC, a football club, the Shillong Chamber Choir, a culture of music... it's all happening here!

LEFT | Seen here are some of the hundreds of menhirs and dolmens erected by the clans that founded the Nartiang village. Megaliths to commemorate important occasions are very much a part of the culture of Meghalaya.

FACING PAGE
A religious procession of the Hajong tribe, who are believed to have migrated from the Hajo area of the Kamrup District of Assam and are now settled in the Garo Hills.

while the ruler is the goddess Ka Blei Nonasynshar Nonghukum. The wave of Christian conversion brought forth the Seng Khasi, a revivalist movement that has been gaining popularity. It was started at the end of the nineteenth century to preserve and promote Khasi culture and is at the forefront of all religious and cultural activities.

Music and dance are the heartbeat of Khasi culture. Ka Shad Suk Mynsiem is the spring festival celebrating harvest and sowing, followed by the Ka Pomblang Nongkrem, a time for thanksgiving. The hugely popular Nongkrem is the crowning glory of all Khasi festivals. Seeking a good harvest and the Almighty's blessings for peace and prosperity, the celebrations around Nongkrem are spread over five days, and religious rituals soon give over to dancing. Every year it is celebrated at Smit village, which is 11 km (7 mi.) from Shillong and is the headquarters of the *syiemkhyrim*, the Khasi council.

Situated at a height of 1,524 m (5,000 ft.) above sea level, Shillong, the capital of Meghalaya, is one of the most picturesque and popular hill stations in the Northeast, taking its name from the Shillong Peak, which dominates the city. There are many legends surrounding this name, the most popular saying that it came from a handsome youth called Shyllong, who was born in mysterious circumstances to a virgin human mother in Bisi, a nearby village. It is believed that he was the Shillong deity and the phrase *kot shillong*, meaning "to bring peace in times of catastrophe (or danger or personal misfortune)", originated in this story. Shillong was the capital of the erstwhile British provincial state of Assam, and remained so even after Independence. Later, when Meghalaya attained full statehood in 1972, Shillong was the natural choice to be the capital of the new state.

Archery is like the state game of the Khasi, enjoying a status way above any other sport. The season, lasting from January to May, abounds with archery contests, and the community thrills to the sound of arrows shot from taut bows. Khasi mythology narrates how Ka-mei-ka-nong-hukum, the Khasi Eve, trained her two sons in the art of archery. She also reined in their impetuous enthusiasm with a stern warning against losing their tempers during a shooting match. Competitions featuring clubs or villages are held frequently. Challenges are issued and each side has men called *nong khan khnam*, who not only act as referees, laying down the rules, but are also believed to know magic incantations to send an opponent's arrows flying wildly off target. The targets, made of grass or the roots of plants, are fastened to poles. Marksmen stand some forty to fifty yards away and the tense anticipation gives way to loud cheering as the arrows head for the target. Betting is very much a part of the fun!

The Khasi Hills are perhaps best known for the township of Sohra, also known as Cherrapunji, geographically famous for once being the wettest place on earth. Cherrapunji is set upon a plateau on the southern slopes of the state. It is dotted with waterfalls cascading over deep gorges. The world's fourth-highest waterfall, the Nohkalikai Falls, comes spectacularly alive in the rains. The major part of the rain in Cherrapunji can be attributed to its orographic characteristics. When the clouds

The passionate pursuit of archery, with the high excitement of betting, has the locals enthralled!

BELOW | The boys dance in the outer circle around the girls at the Nongkrem festivities, ceremonially carrying a sword in one hand and a yak-hair whisk in the other.

FACING PAGE
LEFT | A service is in progress at the All Saints' Cathedral of the Anglican tradition. The foundation stone was laid in 1874 by the then Viceroy of India, Thomas Baring.

RIGHT | Known as the Shillong Cathedral, the Mary Help of Christians Cathedral is built on the site of the first Catholic church constructed in 1913. It has emerged as the main house of worship for the large Catholic populace in the Khasi and Jaintia Hills.

blow over the Khasi Hills from the south, they are funnelled through the valley. The low-flying clouds strike Cherrapunji perpendicularly and are pushed up the steep slopes. It is not surprising, therefore, to find that the heaviest rainfall occurs when the wind blows directly on the Khasi Hills. A notable feature of this monsoon rain is that most of it falls in the morning. Despite such heavy annual rain, Cherrapunji faces acute water shortages and the people living here often have to walk for miles to obtain potable water. Cultivation is hampered by excessive rainfall washing away the topsoil, and though the plateaus are well grassed, the area is fairly rocky. Cherrapunji is also known for its orange groves and orange honey, from which it derives its name.

The area around Cherrapunji is famous for its "living bridges", where over centuries people have mastered the art of knitting roots of trees into large bridges. The process takes ten to fifteen years and the bridges usually last for hundreds of years, the oldest one in use being over 500 years old.

We move onto the Jaintia Hills where traditional Jaintia beliefs tell us the story that in the beginning there were sixteen families who lived in heaven with U Trekirot, the Almighty God, and Ka Syeim Wabooh Wathoo, the goddess queen, who creates living beings. U Trekirot ordered Ka Bei Ram-aw, Mother Earth, to make the world a suitable place for mankind. The *durbar blai*, or assembly of gods, then sent forth seven families to people the earth and made U Lakriah the head of the settlers. Thus commenced the "golden age" of the Jaintia, also known as *pnar* or *syntang*, when man could commune with animals, birds and fish, and there was abundance and righteousness.

From ancient times, the Jaintia Hills were known in the local language as Ka Ri Khadar Dolloi, or "the Land of Twelve Tribal Chiefs", each of whom had his own *elaka*, or area, to govern. The most powerful was the *dolloi*, or king, of Nartiang and on him was bestowed the title of U Kongsan, or Eldest Brother. Whenever there was war, they all came together under his leadership. Later, mounting conflicts made them decide to appoint a king who would oversee the peace. Oral tradition tells us that after a period of searching, U Lakor Singh Sutnga was crowned the first Jaintia king.

The famous Cherrapunji Falls seen during the pre-monsoon season.

The old Khasi belief, which considers the departed as "one[s] chewing betel nut in God's house and for whom uninterrupted betel chewing is the supreme happiness", says everything there is to say about the Khasis' happy bent of mind and the betel nut.

RIGHT
A Jaintia man enjoys a moment of leisure.

Subsequent Jaintia rajas held sway over the tract of flat ground between Sylhet and the Cachar border, plus the area that stretches from the foothills overlooking the Surma Valley to the Kalang River in Nowgong District. The Ahom, who ruled the adjacent Assam region, recorded the exploits of the Jaintia rajas in their *Buranji*, dating to 1500 CE. Prabat Roy, the ruling Jaintia raja, came down from the hills, capturing the southern plains and setting up his capital at Jaintiapur (now in Bangladesh) and establishing the Jaintia Pargana. In the seventeenth century another powerful Jaintia king clashed with the neighbouring Kachari king, seizing the town of Dimaka. Subsequently, when the Kachari king Tamradhwaj was captured by Ram Singh, the Jaintia king, he appealed to the Ahom king Rudra Singha, who promptly invaded and subjugated the Jaintia. Later, they freed themselves but had to seek the help of the British, who held the *diwani* in Sylhet, against the invading Burmese forces. Soon after, however, there was a clash between them over the establishment of an outpost at Nowgong. By 1838, the standoff between the two sides continuing, the British first annexed Jaintia Pargana and then the Jaintia Hills. This ended the reign of Rajendra Singha and the Jaintia kingdom.

The traditional faith of the Jaintia, practised and observed since ancient times is Ka Niamtre, or "the Original Religion". The later Jaintia kings had converted to Hinduism and there is a famous Durga temple at Nartiang village, where the annual Durga Puja is conducted by the villagers. Yet, the local populace continues to perform the rites, rituals and sacrifices passed onto them by their forefathers. Festivals, both religious and secular, play an important part in the life of the community. The Behdeinkhlam festival is the most opulent among them, famous for the high, upright, decorated trees, or *deinkhlam*s. Like so many tribal festivals, it is held to ward off plagues and evil spirits and invoke the blessings of god, as also for a bountiful harvest and overall prosperity. Jowai, the headquarters of the Jaintia Hills District, hosts the festivities and people from far and near gather to participate. Incidentally, some months prior to the festival, people perform rites and sacrifices to bring rain during the Behdeinkhlam as the absence of rain would be a bad omen. On each of the four days of the festival, dancing begins in the morning and continues till evening in the rain and to the music of *ki bhuri*, the tribal flute, *ki ksin,* the drums, *ki bikur*, the trumpets, and *ki chew*, the brass bells.

Jaintia society, having no class and caste division, is egalitarian and thereby is more cohesive. It is matrilineal and matrilocal with a traditional joint family structure in which the maternal uncle manages family affairs. These days they are progressively moving towards a nuclear family structure. Except in politics, women assume an almost equal status to men. Marriage is an elaborate affair, socially approved and arranged.

Vestiges of megaliths are seen scattered all over the Jaintia Hills and this megalithic culture is distinctive of this community. Those located at Nartiang village near Jowai were most likely erected by the clans that founded the village, who also erected hundreds of menhirs and dolmens. Annually, during the religious festival Ka Puja Blai Law, the descendants of the founders of the village place offerings. For a while during the British Raj, the culture of erecting monoliths had lost momentum but it has been revived jointly by cultural organizations like the Seng Khasi and the Seinra.

The Garo tribe, with a population of 862,473 (according to the 2001 census), lives in an area of 8,167 sq km (3,153 sq. mi.) in the Garo Hills. This encompasses three administrative districts, namely West Garo Hills, East Garo Hills and South Garo Hills, with Tura, Williamnagar and Baghmara as their respective headquarters. Rivers Manda, Damring, Ringge, Ganol, Bugi and Simsang form the drainage system of this rain-soaked region. These fast-flowing rivers have necessitated the building of a vast number of bridges, both indigenous and suspension types, often high above the river surface, using material ranging from cane and bamboo to iron and steel.

Tura, the headquarters of the West Garo Hills District is the second largest town in Meghalaya. The name Tura is a British distortion of "Dura" or "Durama", the name of the guardian goddess of the hill range with the Tura Peak, which overlooks the town. Predominantly Garo, the urban population is mainly Baptist Christian and the town is the seat of the Roman Catholic diocese.

The Garo refer to themselves as *achik mande*, or "hill men". They belong to the Tibeto-Burman linguistic group and their closest resemblance, linguistically as well as physically, is to the Kachari. Segmented into two broad classes, as those who live in the hills and those scattered in the plains, eleven regional groups have emerged. Garo villages exist even in the Goalpara and Kamrup

The Behdeinkhlam festival of the Jaintia in all its overpowering grandeur.

FACING PAGE
Soccer is the undisputed king of sports in the Northeast and it all starts here, at the village level, come rain or shine.

Districts of Assam. Traditionally, they were considered a cruel tribe who time and again raided the plains, killing many people and carrying away the heads as trophies.

A matrilineal society, they have three exogamous clans or *septs*—Momin, Marak and Sangma. The unit on which society is based is the *machong*, which quite simply translates into "motherhood". Each *machong* has a common ancestress and is named after an animal, river or cave.

The Garo religion is a mix of the simplest form of Hinduism and pantheism. Tatara-Rabunga is their chief god, closely resembling Brahma. About thirty per cent of the population have converted to Christianity. Many of their ceremonies are connected with

At the gateway of Tura, a Wangala dancer welcomes you to the headquarters of the West Garo Hills.

RIGHT
Dancers accompanied by drums bring alive the much-awaited Wangala festivities of the Garo Hills. Photograph by Somu John Ingty.

crops as they depend mainly on agriculture. Every year, come October–November, the Garo Hills reverberate with the sound of drumbeats that announce to the world the start of Wangala, the most important and much-awaited festival of the Garo people. Also known as Drua Wanbola or Wanma Rongchua, this is the last of the ceremonies to mark the end of the agricultural year—thanksgiving time at the end of the *jhum* cycle. Offerings are made to honour Misi Saljong, the god of fertility, who presides over crops and controls rain, water, and the growth of all things. Drums beat, music flows from flutes, gongs and buffalo-horns, and the village gathers together for seven days and nights of dance, feasting, rice-beer drinking and revelry.

Houses are repaired, new clothes stitched and the village spruced up for the festivities. Animals are kept in stock, the best grain is stored and large vats of beer are brewed. On the first day, the *rugala* ceremony initiates the proceedings. The *nokma*, or chief, puts all the valuable gongs on display. Agricultural implements are placed along the central post of the house. Newly harvested crops are arranged in ritualistic patterns. Then the rice beer is poured over the gongs, food wrapped in plantain leaf is offered as the main sacrificial rite, and blessings of plenty are sought. This is followed by the incense ceremony known as *sasat soa*.

Beginning at the *nokma*'s house, forming two parallel lines, the dancers move through the village, going from house to house. The calendar year of festivities—starting with the Agalmaka festival during the finalising of the *jhum*, followed by the Rongchugala at the first plucking of paddy from the old fields, and then the Ahaia, the inauguration of the plucking of ripened paddy—finds its final expression in the merry-making that follows.

Life in most parts of the Northeast revolves around the day's cooking and, by extension, pigs, both domestic and wild. In most of Meghalaya, it's much the same—no meal is complete without pork. Rice is the staple food and different varieties of rice, ranging from red rice to sticky rice, are cooked in a variety of styles. A particularly popular style of cooking is *jadoh*, where rice and pork are cooked together. *Dohkhlieh*, a pork salad, is also

The interiors of Garo homes show a skillful and ingenious use of bamboo and cane and anything else at hand.

LEFT | Paintings often adorn the beams and rafters.

FACING PAGE
Garo villagers outside their home.

FOLLOWING PAGES
A Wangala dancer, part of the column that moves through the village taking in all the houses.

very popular. Pork in the Garo Hills is generally boiled and cooked with a variety of vegetables. The preparation of boiled pork and red pumpkin, though a bit spicy, was finger-licking delicious! The Khasi and Jaintia also prepare the meat with black sesame seeds that gives it a unique flavour. During the monsoon, the local markets are flooded with a variety of mushrooms, which are cooked together with pork and a dash of bamboo ash water.

On social occasions, the slaughtered animal is generally brought to the cooking venue with appropriate fanfare. Different people then get busy with different aspects of preparation—the stronger men lightly char the carcass over an open fire to burn off the hair while others get busy pounding fistfuls of chilli. Most of the items are cooked wrapped in wild banana leaves or in fresh bamboo cylinders, adding a distinctive fresh green bamboo taste to the food.

The village dormitory system of *nokpante*, or the bachelors' house, acts as the cultural centre for the village. It is here that the boys, yet to be men, learn everything about tradition, acquire dance, music and singing skills, train in the use of weapons and above all the ethics expected from a member of the Garo tribe. The elders provide guidance in citizenship, village administration and the conduct of village life. During festivals the *nokpante* becomes a meeting place for the organisers. Earlier it used to be the centre for planning raids and it was here that headhunters returned with their trophies to celebrate their victories. At the end of a routine day spent in home-related activities, the youth gather here at night and through the laughter and the fun emerges a sense of community, shaping the destiny of a village. Traditional games centred on "trials of strength" are popular among the youth of the *nokpante*. *Wa'pong kal'a*, a kind of cock-fight, is one such game where the contestants are engaged in a tug-of-war. The *gogripa*, or *chagripa*, is a wrestling match fought like a bear-fight and there is a form of rounders called *jakolkala*.

Chilli, rice and pork are essential components of all Garo feasts. Hollow bamboo cylinders, banana leaves and wood fires all add to the distinctive, mouth-watering flavours.

FACING PAGE
One of the many caves that are strung along a 300 km (186 mi.) belt across the southern part of Meghalaya.

Irrespective of which village, tribe or religion a man (or woman) swears allegiance to in the northeastern part of India, football controls his entire sporting sensibilities, quite unlike the rest of the country where cricket rules the roost. As a state, Meghalaya, along with Manipur, has fielded fairly strong soccer teams at the national level. At the grass roots, even in the remotest villages, smartly turned out teams play in front of large rural crowds, and judging from the roars that greet each play into opposing territory, it often sounds like the Durand Cup final!

As we leave Meghalaya, we take a peep at Jadoreng, the inner psycho-physical culture that has been passed down millennia to the Garo from their forefathers. They believe that devoted pursuit of this art enables them to utilize their own *jabirong*, or conscious human psyche. Tapping the latent power of the human mind, psychical transprojection, transmission and transmigration are what Jadoreng is all about. Magic practices such as *tkna nia* or *simania* (divination), *betchalaia*, as in sending a cane after a thief, and the capacity to transform themselves into animals like tigers or elephants, all have a place in this belief system.

The Brahmaputra River

The Garo Hills slope down to the Brahmaputra River, which changes direction at Goalpara and flows in a southern direction into Bangladesh, forming the western boundary of Meghalaya. This narrow corridor is populated by various communities, among whom there is a large population of Muslims who eke out a living from relatively small land holdings along the river. This was the traditional route taken by Mughal forces to invade Assam (Kamrup in those days) from Bengal, until the invading forces were ferociously defeated by the Ahom under the leadership of Lachit Borphukan at the Battle of Saraighat, fought near Guwahati in 1671. The waters themselves cross the international border at Sishumara, from where the Brahmaputra is thenceforth known as the Jamuna.

A *jhum* hut keeps solitary vigil over the lush vegetation in the Tura region.

RIGHT | Members of the Muslim population in Sishumara

FACING PAGE
Life along the Indo-Bangladesh border, where the Brahmaputra rules the daily rhythms.

Tripura

Close to the town of Udaipur in Tripura, Maharaja Dhanyamanikya constructed the temple of the Tripura Sundari in 1501. It is regarded as one of fifty-one *pithasthana*s, or pilgrimage sites, for Hindu pilgrims. According to myth, the toe of the right foot of Mata Sati fell here, and hundreds of thousands of pilgrims offer *puja* here, especially around the festivals of Dussehra and Diwali. There are two identical images of Mata Tripura Sundari inside the temple. The maharajas of Tripura carried with them the smaller, two-foot-tall idol, affectionately called Chhotima, during *mrigaya*, or hunting expeditions, and also during times of war. Tripura Sundari, placed inside the sanctum sanctorum, stands 1.5 m (5 ft.) tall and is made of *kasthi pathar*. Maa Kali is worshipped here in the form of Soroshi. The tortoise shape of the temple has earned it the name of "Kurma Pitha".

Though many believe the former princely state was named after the presiding deity of the land, Tripura Sundari, it is perhaps more likely that the kingdom in ancient times bore the name Tuipra, which means "a land adjoining water". In the days of yore, when the kingdom was flourishing and the ruling dynasties were at their zenith, its boundaries extended up to the Bay of Bengal to its south, the Arakans to the east and the Garo Hills to its north. The British referred to the princely state as the "Hill Tippera State".

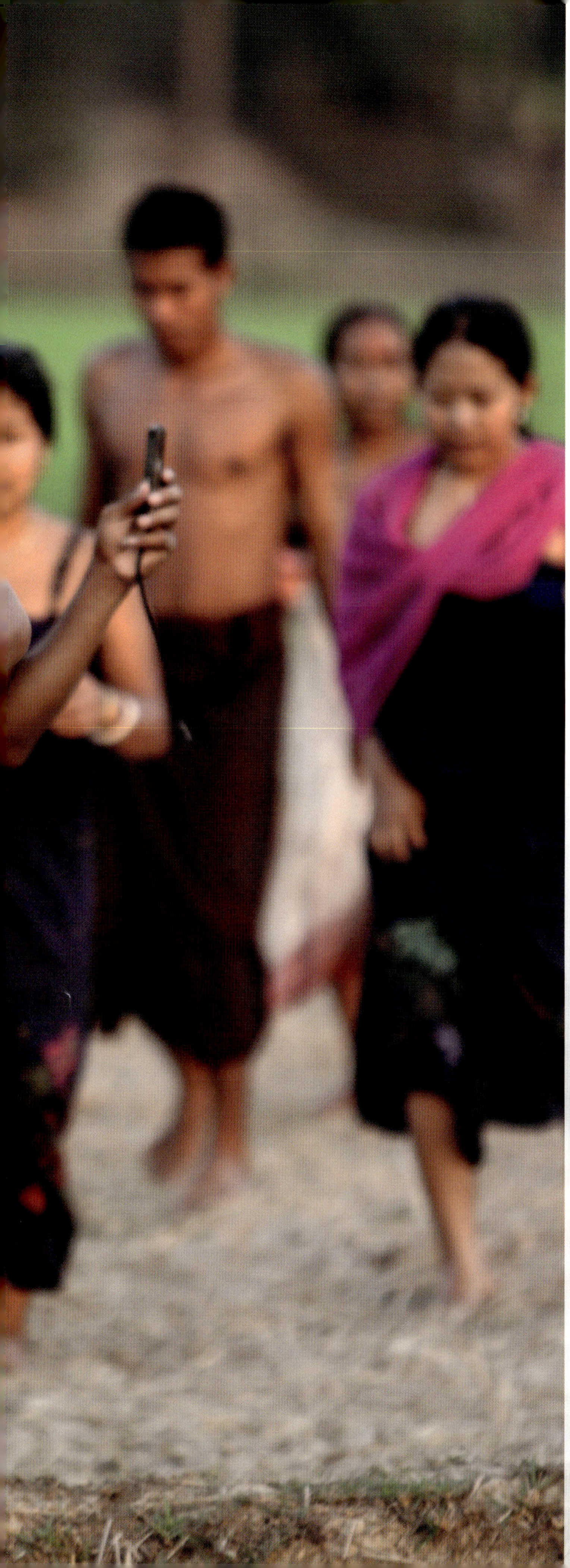

A group of Jamatia tribals; like the other tribes of Tripura they, too, are polytheistic.

The Tripura Sundari enshrined at a temple near Udaipur. This "Kurma Pitha" is regarded as one of the fifty-one *pithasthanas*, or pilgrimage sites, for Hindu pilgrims.

Today, nineteen tribes, together with a large non-tribal Bengali segment, form the population of the state that, over the centuries, has drawn famous personalities, from Huen Tsang to Rabindranath Tagore, to its pristine environs. The capital city of Agartala is mostly populated by Bengalis and their culture and language are at the forefront, with Durga Puja and Saraswati Puja being the main festivals, while native Tripuri festivals, such as Kharchi Puja and Garia Puja, are also celebrated.

History of Tripura

It is evident from the archeological findings of Pilak and Boxnagar that the earliest rulers of Tripura were Buddhists, dating back to the second or third century, though it is not clear who the first Buddhist king was. Buddhism seems to have flourished in Tripura from the second to the ninth centuries. A blend of history and mythology suggests that the Tripura royals were descendants of the "Lunar" dynasty. The mythological prince, Druhyu, the third son of King Yayati of the *Mahabharata*, founded the kingdom of Tribeg. Centuries later, the virtuous King Trilochan's successors settled down in the present state of Tripura. The Hindu maharajas of Tripura were well known as patrons of art and culture. They were addressed as "Dharma Avtar" (Incarnation of Dharma) and as Bobagra or Fa, which mean "Father" in Kokborok, the original language of the people.

Present-day Udaipur, on the banks of the Gomti River, was earlier known as Rangamati and was the capital city of Swadhin Tripura. Maharaja Krishna Kishore Manikya is believed to have shifted the capital to Old Agartala, on the banks of the River Haora in 1760, and renamed it Haveli. Plagued by frequent Kuki raids, and to facilitate better communication with British Bengal, he started the process of shifting the capital from Old Haveli to New Haveli, or present-day Agartala. Maharaja Bir Bikram Manikya Bahadur is regarded as the founder of the planned city of Agartala. The early twentieth century saw the construction of the opulent Ujjayanta Palace at Agartala by Maharaja Radha Kishore Manikya.

Tripura was one of the ancient princely states of the world. According to the *Rajmala* (*Chronicle of Kings*), the kingdom was ruled continuously by as many as 184 Tripuri kings with sovereign and independent status prior to its merger with the Indian Union in 1949. The last king, Bir Bikram Kishore Manikya Bahadur Debbarma, died in 1947, after which the Council of Regency was formed to run the administration under the leadership of Queen

LEFT | A depiction of a royal procession with the Ujjayanta Palace in the background.

RIGHT | The reign of the Tripura kings saw 184 rulers over the centuries.

BELOW LEFT | A devotee plays the flute at a religious festival.

BELOW RIGHT | The Ujjayanta Palace of Agartala gleams in the morning light.

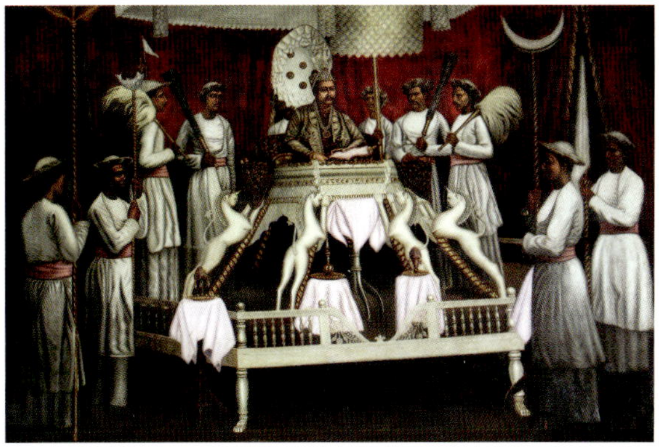

Kanchanprabha Devi, mother of the minor prince, Kirit Bikram. Tripura became a part of the Indian Union on October 15, 1949, when the queen signed the merger agreement.

Towards the end of 1947, Tripura was threatened by Pakistani irregulars who had collected along the newly formed border of East Pakistan with the intention of mounting an offensive on the lines of their invasion of Jammu and Kashmir. This operation started with large-scale infiltration of "non-state" forces into Tripura. Consequently, a special force of the Assam Rifles, under the command of Colonel Sidhiman Rai, was flown to Agartala. They carried out operations against the infiltrators, deterring the main body of Pakistani irregulars from making any further move, and also dealt with communist elements that were trying to link up with their counterparts in East Pakistan.

When Tripura merged into the Indian Union in 1949, the people united to end dynastic rule, joining the umbrella organisation Ganshakti Movement. Post 1947, Tripura has had complicated boundaries; Bangladesh runs along its north, west, south and southeast borders, whereas, in the east, Assam and Mizoram are its immediate neighbours. The creation of East Pakistan (now Bangladesh) severed the railway link between Tripura and the rest of Bengal, adversely affecting the socio-economic scenario in the region. Though the railway connection with Silchar and the rest of Assam has now come into being, the state even today has no immediate link to a major port. The economy of the state is dependent almost entirely on agriculture that, apart from rice, includes jute, sugarcane, wheat, and oil seeds in plenty.

During the twentieth century, no other region in the country has undergone such dramatic changes in its anthropological and demographic history. From a predominantly tribal kingdom with autochthon tribes in the majority, the state became a melting pot of various ethnic groups, today dominated by migrants from Bengal. Besides the ingress of both social and cultural influences, the fertile flatlands in the plains of Tripura also went out of tribal control, creating major economic and other related problems. Bengali influence is seen everywhere in Tripura, from the language to the beliefs and the festivals. Rabindranath Tagore had a special relationship with four successive kings of Tripura. When Tagore was only in his early twenties, Maharaja Birchandra Manikya Bahadur (1862–96), himself an artist, recognised him to be a poet of stature. The association with Tagore had a lasting impact on Tripura's ties with Greater Bengal. The last king, Bir Bikram Kishore Manikya Bahadur Debbarma, conferred the title "Bharat Bhaskar" on Tagore a few months before the latter's death.

Tribes and Culture of Tripura

Hindu, Buddhist and Islamic cultures have converged in Tripura, giving its socio-economic fabric a unique shape. It is considered to be an exciting laboratory of cultural amalgamation. The nineteen tribes of Tripura comprise thirty-one per cent of the population of the state. Among them, the Tripuri, or Deb

LEFT AND FACING PAGE
Regal splendour and pageantry recreated by the artist.

BELOW | Aerial view of the forested Tripura Hills.

The Pilak Sculptures

The plains of Tripura were under the control of several dynasties that ruled in eastern Bengal and Samatata during the ancient period. Some of these were of the Buddhist faith while others were Hindu. Most of the rulers had their capitals in and around the plains bordering the hill areas. For example, the ancient kingdom of Pattikera had its capital in Comilla. Not far from Comilla is Pilak. Sculptures representing this mixed culture, dating back from the ninth to the thirteenth centuries, have been excavated here. In Pilak, the moulded terracotta plaques bear a resemblance to similar statues recovered from Paharpur and Mainamati. The Buddhist Complex is thought to have been built between the ninth and tenth centuries. The art form and style followed in the making of the images and sculptures appear to resemble the style of the Pala and Gupta periods of Bengal. The influence of Arakan art and other local forms is also discernible. In addition, there are a number of rock-cut images and terracotta plaques. Spread over a large area, many of them are yet to be properly identified and labelled.

The eleventh-century statue of Vishnu excavated from Udaipur is part of an important collection that also includes a statue of Bhairava from the Sonamura region; a ninth-century Narsimha avatar, an Avalokitesvara and a Buddha from Pilak; and eleventh-century Uma-Mahesvara, Dandin, Lakshmi and Sarasvati statues from Udaipur. In addition to these, there are some exquisite bronze images dating back to the same period. A miniature ninth-century Vishnu, along with Tara and Ratnasambhava, are examples of the fine and unique craftsmanship of this period.

ABOVE LEFT | A recurrent theme in mythology is that of power and appeasement.

ABOVE RIGHT | Krishna as an incarnation of Vishnu.

CENTRE | Several detailed plaques have been excavated from the site.

BELOW | The Trimurti—Brahma, Vishnu and Shiva.

FACING PAGE
LEFT | Krishna with the *gopis*.

RIGHT | The eleventh-century statue of Vishnu.

Barman, comprise more than half. The Deb Barman are the indigenous tribe of Tripura who ruled for over 2,000 years. With their origins in the Tibeto-Burmese ethnic chain, the Deb Barman are primarily concentrated in the western and northern parts of the state, constituting almost half the tribal population in the area. The standard language of the tribe is Kokborok, which has six dialects spoken in different geographical locations.

Also known as Tipra, the Deb Barman belong to the larger Tripuri community. The Tripuri kings, who belonged to this tribe, brought the acme of Bengali literature and culture to the royal court of Tripura. This became the universal culture of the state. The tribe primarily conforms to the religious beliefs of Hinduism, Vaishnavism and Buddhism, although smaller sects of the rural population also follow Christianity and the traditional aspects of animism. They celebrate a number of festivals like Buddha Jayanti, Pous Sankranti and Kharchi Puja. Dancing, singing and the beating of drums often accompany these religious practices. On the basis of their vocations, the Deb Barman are further sub-divided into a number of clans like the Bachal, Siuk, Koaitoia, Sube Naran, Sena, Jolai, and Khakloo. These clans are called *hadda*s, having their distinct cultural practices and beliefs, including different forms of marriage.

The Reang, or Bru, are the second-largest tribe but some historians consider them to be only a clan of the Tripuri. They are believed to have come to Tripura from the hill tracts of Chittagong and have their own customs and styles of living, and, in addition, they speak the Kau Bru language and not the Kokborok of the Tripuri. The Noatia tribe is a branch of the Tripuri and also uses the Deb Barman name. Their settlements are spread over Tripura and Mizoram. Though they trace their descent from Saint Kashyap, over the past century many have converted to Christianity, especially in Mizoram, and have moved away from their traditional cultural roots.

PREVIOUS PAGES
Trawling the rivers for fish.

The reverberating beat of the *dhol* signals the exhilarating start to most festivities.

The Hojagiri Dance

The Hojagiri dance of the Reang is performed with delicate balance and poise. Silver ornaments—in particular the distinctive coin necklace *rangbauh,* which also indicates a woman's status—have pride of place in their attire. The dance is performed during Lakshmi Puja, which usually falls on the full moon night of Durga Puja. The goddess Mailuma, a form of Lakshmi, is worshipped. The dance is accompanied by the singing of male musicians, who also play the *kham* and the *sumui*. The dancers have to undergo extensive training to perform the deft manoeuvres that involve keeping the upper part of the body motionless to balance various props, while slow hip and waist movements take the audience through the entire story of *jhum* cultivation.

The third-largest tribe are the Kokborok-speaking Jamatia. A staunch Hindu tribe, they are hard-working agriculturists and conscious of their cultural values. They have their own social and administrative structural system. Belonging to Mongolian racial stock, the Jamatia are mostly settled in the western and southern districts of the state. They are a hardy race and are noted for their strength, bravery and skill. In earlier times, they were the most important part of the army, which was called the *jamat*, thereby the name "Jamatia". However, others believe that the name of their community has been derived from the words *jama* and *twia*. While the former means "tax", the latter means "not to bear the burden of". Being soldiers they were exempt from paying tax to the state. Interestingly, the Jamatia had risen in revolt against the ruling monarch in 1863 under their leader Parikshit Jamatia but the rebellion was crushed.

They conduct their social and religious activities as guided by their highest council, the Jamatia *hoda*. They perform Ganga Puja, Garia Puja, the Bolong Suwamani and Lakshmi Puja with fervour to invoke the blessings of the various gods and

PRESENT AND FACING PAGE
The Reang tribe displays much dignity in the face of the hardships of displacement.

PRESENT AND FACING PAGE
Morning ablutions on a *puja* day. The Jamatia observe several *pujas*, including the Ganga Puja, Goria Puja, Bolong Suwamani and Lakshmi Puja.

goddesses for the welfare of the family and society. Baba Goria is the universal god of all indigenous Tripuri. Like the other tribes of Tripura, the Jamatia are also polytheistic. They worship about fourteen gods, among whom the most prominent are the Mwtai Kotor, Twima and Goria Mwtai.

All the religious rituals are performed by the *okra*, the head priest of the clan. The *moyal* are the sixteen regions into which the entire clan is divided. Each *moyal* is headed by a *panchai* for a period of five years. Then there is the *luku*, or village level, whose chief is called the *chokdiri* and is selected by the head of each family of the village for a period of five years. In turn, the *chokdiri* and a few village elders select the *panchai*. The *okra* is selected by the *chokdiri*s and the *panchai*s. Nowadays, the apex body is constituted by two *hoda okras*. The *hoda* is responsible for resolving disputes in their community while also working towards the development of society and preserving the traditional culture of the Jamatia.

Throughout its history, the Northeast has seen waves of refugees flee from neighbouring regions and from within. The escapees from Tibet in the 1950s, the Chakma from East Pakistan in 1964, the 1971 Bangladesh exodus, and, more recently, the Reang, who were dislocated from Mizoram and continue to live in refugee camps in the Kanchanpur sub-division of North Tripura. Whatever the reason, the displacement of any large human population is tragic in the extreme. Ethnic clashes and persecution by the Mizo forced the Reang to leave their homes in Mammit and Longlei Districts. Thirty-five thousand of them took refuge in the North Tripura District in late 1997 and they languish in camps that have since claimed several lives. They continue to await a solution, waiting to return home.

Unakoti

Situated in North Tripura District, Unakoti dates back to the seventh to ninth centuries. The word *unakoti* means "one less than a crore (ten million)". Legend has it that Shiva and His accompanying gods and goddesses, together totaling one crore, rested at this spot on their way to Kashi. At sunrise, none of them awoke in time and Shiva, enraged, cursed them, turning them into stone and leaving by Himself. The central Shiva head is known as Unakotiswara Kal Bhairav. Thousands of pilgrims flock to Unakoti in April when the Ashokastami Mela is held.

Among the local populace, there is also the story of a sculptor named Kallu Kumar, who was a devotee of Shiva and Parvati and dearly wanted to accompany them to Kailash Parvat. To humour Parvati, Shiva agreed to take Kumar along but on the condition that the man must sculpt one crore images of Shiva in one night. Despite working at breakneck speed, at the crack of dawn Kumar was short of the target by just one.

Mizoram

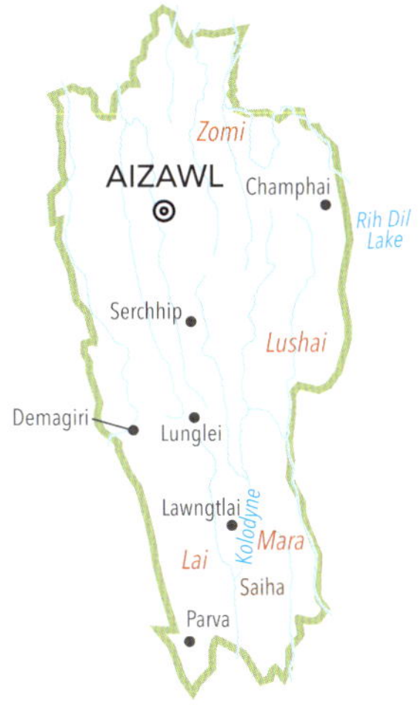

The amiable Mizo takes much pride in the land of his forefathers, and with good reason! Breathtaking vistas greet the eye wherever the gaze travels. Especially during the monsoon, the Mizo Hills come alive and the flora and fauna are a visual delight. Miles upon miles of bamboo intermixed with other vegetation types, especially when viewed from above, resemble green tresses that envelop the hillsides. Mizoram's tropical location, together with the altitude, makes for a mild climate throughout the year.

Assam lies to the north, Tripura to the west, and Manipur to the northeast, while Mizoram also shares international borders with Bangladesh to the west and Myanmar to the east. A host of rivers and their tributaries drain the Mizo Hills. The majestic Kaladan River, or Kolodyne, also known as the Chhimtuipui Lui in the Mizo language, is the biggest river of the region. The river, in fact, originates in the Chin state of Myanmar, flows into South Mizoram and then flows back into Myanmar and the Kolodyne Project that is underway between the two neighbours, holds many promises for the future. The Tlawng, Tut, Tuirial and the Tuivawl system of rivers flows northwards to join the Barak River in the Cachar District of Assam. The Karnaphuli, or Khawthlang Tuipui, and its tributaries drain the western part of the state. Many important towns have come up at the mouth of the river,

Flying into Mizoram from Imphal, heading for the capital city Aizawl, we cross a small village not far from the town of Vairengte that houses CIJWS, the Counter-Insurgency and Jungle Warfare School.

including Chittagong in Bangladesh. Before Independence the river routes were the highways connecting Mizoram to the rest of India via Cachar in the north and Chittagong in the south.

The Palak, situated in southern Mizoram, is the biggest lake in the state. It is believed to have been created by an earthquake where resultant landslides submerged a village whose underwater ruins are visible even today, the houses and huts still intact in their watery grave. A hundred-odd kilometres (about 60 mi.) from Aizawl is the Tamdil Lake. Legend would have us believe that a huge mustard plant once grew here. When the plant was cut down, jets of water sprayed from the plant and a pool of water was formed. Tamdil Lake, "Lake of the Mustard Plant", is a major tourist attraction today. The Rih Dil is the most significant lake for the Mizo but it is now located within Myanmar. It is believed that the souls of those who die pass through this lake on their way to heaven.

The Mizo code of ethics or dharma, called *tlawamngaihna*, highlights self-sacrifice and service to others and is a strong moral force in the lives of the people. This is a close-knit society with no class or sex discrimination. The Mizo are believed to be Mongolian in origin, migrating into India from China. The first Mizo who settled in India were known as the Kuki and later immigrants were called the New Kuki. Tribes of several ethnic groups, linked either culturally or linguistically, form the Lushai or Lusei, with Mizo being the umbrella term that brings two-thirds of the populace together. There is also an attempt to unite all Mizo wherever they live including the Hmar, Mara, Paite, Lai and Ralte, among others. There are also the sub-tribes of the Tripuri and the Reang settled in Western Mizoram. This region is home to the Chakma, a predominantly Buddhist tribe of Arakanese origin as well.

The Lai youth of Lawngtlai catch their breath between dances.

FACING PAGE
Rih Dil Lake, which is of great importance to the Mizo, in fact stands three kilometres (2 mi.) into Myanmar, another casualty to careless formation of boundary lines.

History of Mizoram from Colonisation to Today

As the British Empire expanded eastwards along the Chittagong axis, the Mizo were among the last bastion to finally crumble. In 1865–68, Kuki and Lushai raiding parties from the southern hills carried out a number of attacks in the Cachar area to put a stop to the looming threat and immediately the British mounted retaliatory expeditions but at first could not penetrate far afield. It was in the winter of 1871 that a series of military operations were undertaken to subjugate the Lushai tribes. Two columns moved in from different points: one from Silchar southwards, to punish the tribes on the northeast corner, near the border with Manipur; and the other from Chittagong eastwards, to punish the tribes based at Aizawl and Lunglei. Although the two columns failed to meet, they both achieved their objective. Large numbers of tribesmen made their submission, particularly the Howlong clan around Aizawl, and the Lushai gave no further trouble to the British for a few years. About a hundred personnel of the Frontier Police were awarded the India General Service Medal with the clasp "Looshai" for this operation—the first such award to be recorded in the Northeast during the Raj.

Chronicling the events and articulating British policy, G. Wood Thorpe of the Royal Engineers wrote in *The Lushai Expedition, 1871–1872*, in the familiar tone of the colonialist of the day:

> The North-eastern frontier of India has ever been a fruitful source of trouble and expense to the Government of this Empire. The history of each district on this frontier, whether prior or subsequent to its annexation as a portion of British territory, is almost the same. Bordered by or forming part of hill districts, inhabited by fierce and predatory tribes forever making raids on their neighbours' villages, burning and plundering them, and carrying off the inhabitants, it was not to be supposed that those under our protection should escape.

The incident of the kidnapping of Mary Winchester in 1871 proved to be the turning point that brought the British firmly into the region. In 1887 the government in Calcutta decided to survey the border with the Chin Hills with the view of extending British territory up to the Burmese border. By 1891, South Lushai Hills was constituted a district of the Chittagong Division.

The Mizo are an affable people and carry forward their vibrant culture with enthusiasm.

ABOVE RIGHT AND BELOW | Scenes from the Lushai expeditions, launched by the British over two decades from 1871 to 1891 to subjugate the Lushai tribes.

FACING PAGE
After the Lushai expeditions, the British installed themselves in the Mizo Hills, constituting the South Lushai Hills District in 1891 as a part of the Chittagong Division.

Traditionally animistic like most tribal communities, Mizoram is now predominantly Christian. Certain tribes retain their animism while others have adopted a fusion of spiritual practices, like the mainly nomadic Chakma who combine Hinduism, Buddhism and animism. The Khan seem to have incorporated the culture of the Puy of ancient Srikshetra, the Hindu kingdom of Myanmar.

The advent of the Christian missionaries during the nineteenth century brought about radical change in the social framework of the region. Traditional beliefs and practices prevalent were completely swept aside by the acceptance of the Gospel. The tribal belief of the Mizo was based on the concept of a supreme power called Pathian, who was worshipped by performing various religious, sacrificial and other ceremonies. Besides this, there were also certain animistic practices in the region that involved offering sacrifices to evil spirits for healing any kind of spiritual or physical illness. Due to such rituals, the Western missionaries tagged the traditional Mizo religion as heathenism or, in other words, an uncivilised culture. In 1871, eight-year-old Mary Winchester was abducted by a raiding party under the chieftain, Chawma, and taken to a place near Serchhip, subsequently to be rescued a year later by British forces. Mary Winchester in later years was given the status of a "guiding light" because of whom the people of Mizoram emerged from the "dark ages". Sociologists also believe that extreme violence in the past had deeply impacted and scarred the Mizo psyche and so the society was ripe for missionaries to preach the gospel. Religiosity being a part of the Mizo ethos and sensibility, plus

the inherent social code of conduct that is a way of life played its role. However, the Mizo today believe that although their former way of life was far from being perfect, this critical assessment of their culture was inappropriate.

The first European missionary in the region, William Williams, arrived in the Lushai Hills in March 1881 from the Khasi Hills and within twelve years mass conversions had started. It took the entire Mizo community barely fifty years to embrace the doctrines of the new religion completely. The primary denomination in the Mizo Hills is by far Presbyterian while many other churches have mushroomed over the years.

Prior to the arrival of the missionaries, there was no written script and very little difference in the spoken dialects of the Lushai spread across various villages. In 1893 the Arthington Aborigines Mission sent two missionaries, James Herbert Lorrain and Frederick William Savidge, to Aizawl, both of whom later based themselves at Lunglei. They learnt the language, and were together instrumental in converting the Duhlien language of the Lushai to the Roman script. They translated parables from the Bible while producing a "Lusie-English" dictionary. Mission schools immediately began to teach people how to read and write. The Gospel of St. John and Acts of the Apostles were then translated into Lushai/ Duhlien. The Synod Press was established in 1911 and in the next five years the entire New Testament had been published in translation.

During the process of the handover of power by the British, the people of Aizawl were in favour of joining the Union of India. This wish had been expressed once before, when in the early 1920s the citizens had asked for the inclusion of the Lushai Hills in the Government of India Reform Act of 1919; the petitioners had been promptly jailed! In 1946 the Mizo Union was formed and on August 15, 1947, it had sent its formal assent to the Governor of Assam that the Mizo Hills should remain a part of the state. Part of the Mizo Union's agenda, along with church leaders, was to curb the unlimited powers conferred on the tribal chiefs by the British, with a view towards introducing democratic reforms. This set the chiefs against the Mizo Union and they became the rallying point for the radicals in the countryside. The last two British superintendents of the Lushai Hills, however, had unofficially sowed the seeds of discontent. Anthony Gilchrist McCall, whose tenure coincided with the war years, had suggested to the Lushai-Chin clans of India and Burma that they

Ingenuity is often a hallmark of the young, anywhere in the world.

TOP | Major Sailo of the Assam Rifles sits in front of the plaque commemorating Mary Winchester.

PRESENT PAGE
Christianity dominates in the Mizo Hills, with Presbyterianism being the primary denomination among many.

settle for a separate mountain state outside the Indian Union under a League of Nations trusteeship; his successor, A.R.H. MacDonald, advised that the Lushai Hills remain a protectorate of Great Britain after the Indian subcontinent was partitioned.

Having decided to stay with the Indian Union, the Mizo Union rebuffed all approaches by Phizo and other Naga radicals who visited them with the proposal that they join hands for the demand of political independence. The Mizo Union, with the people solidly behind them, stuck to their stance that they be given a separate Mizo state within India. In 1954, Pu Laldenga returned to Aizawl after having served in the Army. Opposed to the liberal outlook of the elders, he soon became the rallying point for the radicals who were also encouraged by exaggerated accounts of Naga success in the jungles to the north. Four years later, the dreaded 50-year cyclical famine, *mautum*, caused by the flowering of bamboo and the subsequent invasion of rats, gave Laldenga the platform he needed, and the Mizo National Famine Front was launched. Later, the word "Famine" was dropped from its name.

By 1965, over 10,000 Mizo had been extensively trained in the Chittagong Hill Tracts by Pakistan and organized into a cohesive army, armed with rifles, light machine guns and mortars. The MNF declared independence for Mizoram in February 1966.

Over the next decade or so, the Lushai Hills saw some bitter and sustained fighting between the MNF and the Assam Rifles, the Indian Army and the Border Security Force.

In 1986 the historic Memorandum of Settlement was signed between the Government of India and the Mizo National Front. Subsequently, Mizoram gained statehood in 1987, becoming the twenty-third state of India. The capital at Aizawl has the Mizoram State Legislative Assembly with 40 seats. One Member of Parliament represents the state in the Lok Sabha and Rajya Sabha. Vast constitutional, political and administrative changes have been put in place. The eight district and regional councils take the place of the traditional chieftainship. Today the Lai, Mara and Chakma have separate autonomous district councils. The village councils are the grass roots of democracy in Mizoram.

The People and Culture of Mizoram

Over eighty-eight per cent of Mizo farmers are engaged in the traditional slash and burn form of cultivation. The remaining twelve per cent practise wet rice cultivation. Almost all biodiversity strategy and action plans are focussed on adopting and popularising modified shifting cultivation practices for conservation. This is a burning issue for the Northeast as an expanse of 3,869 sq km (1,493 sq. mi.) is used for *jhumming* each

LEFT AND BELOW | *Jhumming* fires ravage the hillsides annually. When the smoke clears, the countryside is scarred by huge, bald patches, which are increasingly difficult to recover from.

FACING PAGE
LEFT | Pu Laldenga, the self-styled president of the Mizo National Front (MNF).

RIGHT | Gun-toting rebels pose for a photo.

Birds are easy prey for humans. A common sight even at roadside stalls.

FACING PAGE
Habitat destruction and rampant hunting is rapidly bringing living creatures, be they freshwater crabs or porcupines, to the brink of extinction.

year and almost 450,000 households earn their livelihood from it. As a majority of the indigenous tribes are engaged in this form of cultivation, the adverse impact on the environment and biodiversity is undeniable. The debate still rages on while more and more stripped hillsides give the lie to a seemingly rich part of the country, bringing even birds and animals to the brink of extinction.

Once Mizoram was home to animals, birds and humans alike but over the years the former two are dwindling in number and diversity at an accelerating pace. The ever-increasing pressure of population brings greater habitat destruction as more and more land is subjected to repeated cutting and burning for *jhum* cultivation. Add to this excessive and rampant hunting and the fauna face an uncertain future. Urgent measures need to be taken to prevent a scenario of silent forests!

Historically, the Lai people are descended from the Chin community of Burma. One of their major clans is the Pawi. The word "Pawi" comes from the Duhlien word *pawte* that means "leopard". Among the earliest settlers in the state, they migrated to the Lushai Hills in the eighteenth century, settling in what is today the Lawngtlai District. Like many other ethnic tribes, the Lai are also anxious to protect their culture, language and traditional way of living. Accordingly they established the Lai Autonomous District Council (LADC) in 1972 with their headquarters in the town of Lawngtlai. Governing a total population of around seventy thousand as of 2008, the LADC is one of the three autonomous district councils in Mizoram.

The Lai are patrilineal in descent, tracing the family line through the males. The eldest son generally inherits the entire property. As a community, there are strong social obligations that make it incumbent on parents to look after their children, while the children in turn look after their aged parents. Lai women enjoy a high social status in society and are known to be hard-working. Both men and women work together in *jhum* fields. Many of their ancient traditions are preserved in myriad folktales, songs and dances.

Formerly known as "Lakher", the Mara are indigenous people belonging to the Kuki clan of the Tibeto-Burman family. They moved from their original home in southern China via the Chin Hills to present-day Maraland by the seventeenth century. The Mara form one of the three autonomous district councils

Mara dancers from Saiha.

TOP RIGHT | Cheraw, the famous bamboo dance of sanctification and redemption.

RIGHT | Drumbeats, gongs, and clapping accompany the vigorous song and dance and the *khlak-khlak* of the bamboos!

PREVIOUS PAGES
Lawngtlai.

within the state. In fact, Saiha, the headquarters of Chhimtuipui District, situated in the south-central part of the state, has the highest concentration of the tribe and is also the commercial hub of the Mara community. In 1945, a conference was convened in Saikao at a time when India was striving for independence. The Lushai Hills were in a state of political turmoil—the Mara chiefs demanding the establishment of a separate administrative unit, as they did not want to be under the direct control of the Lushai Hills District.

Almost all ethnic Mara in the Saiha District are Christians. The physical distance, even from Aizawl, and the lack of proper communication, agricultural and economic facilities have resulted in a sense of alienation and isolation. Despite all odds, the Mara are known to be a dedicated people, continually struggling to sustain the identity and unique cultural heritage of their community.

The Chapchar Kut, Mim Kut and Pawl Kut festivals are major landmarks in a calendar year. Pork is the all-time favourite of the Mizo, and as among many communities of the Northeast, the highlight of many festivals. The quantity of pork consumed annually is worth well over Rs. 100 crore ($14,000,000 USD) and about eighty per cent has to be imported. All the three Kuts, Chapchar Kut, Mim Kut, Pawl Kut, as well as a fourth, Thalfavang Kut, are connected with agricultural phases and the feasting and dancing go on for days. On the first day of the Chapchar Kut, celebrated at the end of the harvest, pigs are killed in huge quantities by the members of the chief's clan for the feast given by him. By the end of the day much pork will be eaten, and *zu*, or rice beer, will be drunk. On the second day the other clans of the village will kill their pigs for the village feast. Some popular pork dishes are *vawksa rep*, or smoked pork, and pork stew with spinach and bamboo shoot, or *bai*.

The Chakma are one of the largest tribes inhabiting the Chittagong Hill Tracts in Bangladesh and the western ranges of Mizoram. They are followers of Theravada Buddhism, and have their own distinct culture, folklore, literature and traditions. At the time of Independence they expected the region to become a part of India but instead the area was given to East Pakistan. This created widespread resentment as the Buddhist Chakma considered themselves culturally similar to the Hindu population of India. Even after the formation of Bangladesh they have continued to be persecuted.

L&T-KOMATSU

LEFT | A woman from the Chakma Hills.

BELOW | The road between Aizawl and Lunglei being constructed with World Bank aid.

FACING PAGE
The Kolodyne River Project.

Before 1947, the southern part of Mizoram was directly connected to the port city of Chittagong, with trade plying from Lunglei through the Chakma Hills. Once the area was partitioned, the entire equation changed, with Mizoram getting cut off from all sides; in terms of physical distance, it became the remotest Indian region. Addressing this issue, the Kolodyne River Project is of great significance to the entire Northeast. Primarily it will result in better connectivity with Southeast Asia and also the rest of the world, thereby addressing the country's relatively new "Look East Policy".

In April 2009, a bilateral agreement was signed between the governments of India and Myanmar for constructing a trade route along the course of the Kolodyne (Chhimtuipui) River. As a result, a project for developing a multi-modal transit and transport facility on the river has started. This proposes to connect Mizoram with the Sittwe Port of Myanmar and once again give the region direct access to the Bay of Bengal. The Kolodyne River, being the biggest waterway in the Mizo Hills, debouches into Myanmar. It is then navigable beyond Kaletwa to its merger point with the Bay of Bengal at Sittwe, which has traditionally been an important port for the export of rice from Myanmar. India's export relations with its eastern neighbour have improved significantly—it now stands as Myanmar's fourth-largest trade partner, after China, Thailand and Singapore.

Bibliography

A Short Guide to Koch Bihar Palace Museum. Kolkata: Archaeological Survey of India.

Cultural Pride of Meghalaya: Dances and Festivals. Shillong: Directorate of Information and Public Relations, Government of Meghalaya, 2002.

Dwellers of the High Hills—The Khasis of Meghalaya. Shillong: Directorate of Information and Public Relations, Government of Meghalaya, 2002.

Excavation at Rajpat Mound 1998–2000. Kolkata: Archaeological Survey of India.

Meghalaya—Flora and Fauna. Shillong: Directorate of Information and Public Relations, Government of Meghalaya, 2002.

The Pristine Culture and Society of the Garos of Meghalaya. Shillong: Directorate of Information and Public Relations, Government of Meghalaya, 2002.

Allen, Charles. *Duel in the Snows: The True Story of the Younghusband Mission to Lhasa*. London: John Murray, 2004.

Athickal, Joseph. *Maram Nagas: A Socio-Cultural Study*. New Delhi: Mittal Publications, 1992.

Atreya, Harka Bahadur Chhetri. *The Bodos in Assam: A Socio-Cultural Study 2005–2006*. Kolkata: Maulana Abul Kalam Azad Institute of Asian Studies, 2007.

Bareh, H. M. *Encyclopaedia of North-East India: Arunachal*. New Delhi: Mittal Publications, 2001.

Bareh, H. M. *Encyclopaedia of North-East India: Assam*. New Delhi: Mittal Publications, 2001.

Bareh, H.M. *Encyclopaedia of North-East India: Manipur*. New Delhi: Mittal Publications, 2001.

Bareh, H. M. *Encyclopaedia of North-East India: Meghalaya*. New Delhi: Mittal Publications, 2001.

Bareh, H. M. *Encyclopaedia of North-East India: Mizoram*. New Delhi: Mittal Publications, 2001.

Bareh, H. M. *Encyclopaedia of North-East India: Nagaland*. New Delhi: Mittal Publications, 2001.

Bareh, H. M. *Encyclopaedia of North-East India: Sikkim*. New Delhi: Mittal Publications, 2001.

Bareh, H. M. *Encyclopaedia of North-East India: Tripura*. New Delhi: Mittal Publications, 2001.

Bandopadhyay, Sruti. *Manipuri Dance: An Assessment on History and Presentation*. New Delhi: Shubhi Publications, 2010.

Banerjee, Bikash. *The Bokars: An Anthropological Research on their Ecological Settings and Social Systems*. Arunachal Pradesh: Directorate of Research, Government of Arunachal Pradesh, 1999.

Barua, Harakanta. *Asama Buranji: A History of Assam from the Commencement of Ahom Rule to the British Occupation 1826*. Assam: Dept. of Historical and Antiquarian Studies, 1962.

Baruah, Sanjib. *India Against Itself: Assam and the Politics of Nationality*. Philadelphia: University of Pennsylvania Press, 1999.

Baruah, Swarna Lata. *Last Days of the Ahom Monarchy: A History of Assam from 1769–1826*. New Delhi: Munshiram Memorial Publishers, 1993.

Basu, Nirmal Kumar. *Assam in the Ahom Age, 1228–1826*. Kolkata: Sanskrit Pustak Bhandar, 1970.

Begi, Joram. *Education in Arunachal Pradesh Since 1947: Constraints, Opportunities, Initiatives and Needs*. New Delhi: Mittal Publications, 2007.

Behera, M. C., and S. K. Chaudhuri. *Indigenous Faith and Practices of the Tribes of Arunachal Pradesh*. New Delhi and Itanagar: Himalayan Publishers, 1998.

Bhalla, Dipti and Shiv Kunal Verma. *East of Kanchendzonga (Northeast Trilogy-I)*. Gurgaon: KaleidoIndia, 2012.

Bhalla, Dipti and Shiv Kunal Verma. *Brahma's Creation (Northeast Trilogy-II)*. Gurgaon: KaleidoIndia, 2012.

Bhalla, Dipti and Shiv Kunal Verma. *Children of the Dawn (Northeast Trilogy-III)*. Gurgaon: KaleidoIndia, 2012.

Bhargava, Gopal K., and S. C. Bhatt. *Land & People of Indian States & Union Territories*. New Delhi: Kalpaz Publications, 2006.

Bhushan, Chandra. *Assam: Its Heritage and Culture*. New Delhi: Kalpaz Publications, 2005.

Blackburn, Stuart. *Himalayan Tribal Tales: Oral Tradition and Culture in the Apatani Valley*. Netherlands: Koninklijke Brill, 2002.

Bogle, George, and Thomas Manning. *Narratives of the Mission of George Boggle to Tibet: And of the Journey of Thomas Manning to Lhasa*. London: Barnes & Noble, 1923.

Bose, Manilal. *History of Arunachal Pradesh*. New Delhi: Concept Publishing Company, 1997.

Bower, Ursula Graham. *Drums Behind The Hill*. New York: William Morrow & Co., 1950.

Bower, Ursula Graham. *Naga Path*, London: John Murray, 1950.

Chakrabarti, D. K. *The Issues in East Indian Archaeology*. New Delhi: Munshiram Manoharlal Publishers Pvt Ltd., 1998.

Chatterjee, Suhas. *Mizoram Encyclopaedia* (3 Volumes). New Delhi: Jaico Publishing House, 1990.

Chisti, S. M. A. W. *Political Development in Manipur:1919–1949*, New Delhi: Gyan Publishing House, 2005.

Chowdhury, Jyotirindra Nath. *The Tribal Culture and History of Arunachal Pradesh*. New Delhi: Daya Publishing House, 1990.

Chutia, Ram Chandra. *Nyishi Customs, Folklore and Language*. New Delhi: Spectrum Publications, 2006.

Dai, Mamang. *Arunachal Pradesh: The Hidden Land*. New Delhi: Sky Prints Pvt. Ltd, 2002.

Dalvi, J. P. *Himalayan Blunder: The Curtain-Raiser to the Sino-Indian War in 1962*, Dehradun: Natraj Publishers, 1997.

Das, Shiva Tosh. *Life Style Indian Tribes: Locational Practice* (3 Volumes). New Delhi: Gian Publishing House, 1989.

Das, Sujoy, and Arundhati Ray. *Sikkim: A Traveller's Guide*. New Delhi: Permanent Black, 2001.

Datta-Ray, B., and S. P. Agrawal. *Reorganisation of Northeast India Since 1947*. New Delhi: Concept Publishing Company, 1994.

Deka, Kanak Sen. *Assam's Crisis: Myth and Reality*. New Delhi: Mittal Publications, 1993.

Deori, Saranan. *Religious Practices of the Deoris*. Guwahati: Bina Library, 2002.

Dev, B. J., and D. K. Lahiri. *Assam Muslims: Politics and Cohesion*. New Delhi: Mittal Publications, 1985.

Dhasmana, M. M. *The Ramos of Arunachal*. New Delhi: Concept Publishing Company, 1979.

Elwin, Verrier. *A Philosophy for NEFA*. Itanagar: Directorate of Research, Government of Arunachal Pradesh, 1958.

Elwin, Verrier. *The Tribal World of Verrier Elwin*. New York: Oxford University Press, 1964.

Elwin, Verrier. *A New Book of Tribal Fiction*. Shillong: North-East Frontier Agency, 1970.

Elwin, Verrier. *Nagaland*. New Delhi: Spectrum Publications, 1997.

Fürer-Haimendorf, Christoph von. *Naked Nagas*. London: Methuen & Co. Ltd, 1939.

Fürer-Haimendorf, Christoph von. *Himalayan Barbary*. London: John Murray (Publishers) Ltd., 1955.

Fürer-Haimendorf, Christoph von. *The APA Tanis and Their Neighbours*. London: Routledge, 1962.

Fürer-Haimendorf, Christoph von. *Highlanders of Arunachal Pradesh: Anthropological Research in North-East India*. New Delhi: Vikas Publishing House, 1982.

Fürer-Haimendorf, Christoph von. *Tribes of India: The Struggle for Survival*. Berkeley, CA: University of California Press, 1982.

Fürer-Haimendorf, Christoph von. *Tribal Populations and Cultures of the Indian Subcontinent*. Leiden: E J Brill, 1985.

Gait, Edward Albert. *A History of Assam*. London: Thacker, Spink & Co., 1906.

Gan-Chaudhury, Jagadis. *An Anthology of Tripura*, New Delhi: Inter-India Publications, 1985.

Gee, E. P. *The Wildlife of India*, New Delhi: Harper Collins, 1964.

Ghosh, G. K., and Shukla Ghosh. *Women of Manipur*. New Delhi: APH Publishing Corporation, 1997.

Ghosh, G. K. *Bamboo: The Wonderful Grass*. New Delhi: APH Publishing Corporation, 2008.

Gogoi, Lila. *The History of the System of Ahom Administration*. Kolkata: Punthi Pustak, 1991.

Gogoi, Nitul Kumar. *Continuity and Change Among the Ahom*. New Delhi: Concept Publishing Company, 2006.

Gogoi, Sangeeta, and Manjil Hazarika, eds. *Mong Kham*. Guwahati: 1st International Me-Dam Me-Phi Celebration Committee, 2010.

Gohain, Chowkhamoon. *The Tai Khamtis*, Chowkham (NEFA), 1971.

Grimwood, Ethel St Clair. *My Three Years in Manipur and Escape From the Recent Mutiny*. London: Richard Bentley & Son, 1891.

Guha, Amalendu. *Planter-Raj to Swaraj: Freedom Struggle and Electoral Politics in Assam, 1826–1947*. Indian Council of Historical Research. New Delhi: People's Publishing House, 1977.

Gulia, Kuldip Singh. *Human Ecology of Sikkim: A Case study of Upper Rangit Basin*. New Delhi: Kalpaz Publications, 2005.

Hamilton, Angus. *In Abor Jungles of North-East India*. New Delhi: Mittal Publications, 1983.

Hlychho, John Hamlet. *The Maras: Head-hunters to Soul-hunters*. New Delhi: Indian Society for Promoting Christian Knowledge, 2009.

Hlychho, P. T. *Maraland: Yesterday and Today*. Shillong: PT Hlychho, 2007.

Hodson, Thomas Callan. *The Naga Tribes of Manipur*. London: Macmillan & Co., 1911.

Hutton, J. H. *The Angamai Nagas, With Some Notes on Neighbouring Tribes*. London: Macmillan & Co., 1921.

Hutton, J. H. *The Sema Nagas*, London: Macmillan & Co., 1921.

Joshi, H. G. *Arunachal Pradesh: Past and Present*. New Delhi: Mittal Publications, 2005.

Joshi, Hargovind. *Arunachal Pradesh: Past and Present*. New Delhi: Mittal Publications, 2005.

Joshi, Hargovind. *Mizoram: Past and Present*. New Delhi: Mittal Publications, 2005.

Kapadia, Harish, and Geeta Kapadia. *Into the Untravelled Himalaya: Travels, Treks and Climbs*. New Delhi: Indus Publishing, 2005.

Khullar, D. K. *When Generals Failed: The Chinese Invasion*. New Delhi: Manas Publications, 1999.

Kingdon-Ward, Frank. *Land of the Blue Poppy*. London: Cambridge University Press, 1913.

Kingdon-Ward, Frank. *Mystery Rivers of Tibet*. London: Seeley Service & Co., 1923.

Kingdon-Ward, Frank. *Plant Hunting at the Edge of the World*. London: Victor Gollancz Ltd., 1930.

Kri, Hakraso, *The Mishmis: An Introduction*. Tinsukia: The City Press, 2008.

Kumar, B. B. *Naga Identity*. New Delhi: Concept Publishing Company, 2005.

Lalrimawia. *Mizoram: History & Cultural Identity*. New Delhi: Spectrum Publications, 1995.

Lalthlengliana, C. *Lushai Hills: Annexation, Resistance & Pacification. 1886–1898*. New Delhi: Akanksha Publishing House, 2007.

Lamb, Alsatair. *McMahon Line: Hardinge and the Simla Conference*. London: Routledge & K Paul, 1966.

Lamb, Alastair. *British India and Tibet, 1766–1910*. London: Taylor & Francis, 1986.

Mandal, Ramkrishna, and Minto Ete. *Women in North East India: Role and Status of Arunachal Women*. New Delhi: Mittal Publications, 2010.

Mackintosh, L. J. *Birds of Darjeeling and India*. Kolkata: JN Banerjee & Son, 1915.

McKay, Alex. *Tibet and the British Raj: The Frontier Cadre, 1904–1947*. Surrey: Curzon Press, 1997.

Mibang, Tamo, and M. C. Behera. *Marriage in Tribal Societies: Cultural Dynamics and Social Realities*. Kolkata: Maulana Abul Kalam Azad Institute of Asian Studies, 2007.

Mibang, Tamo, and Sarit Kumar Chaudhuri. *Understanding Tribal Religion*. New Delhi: Mittal Publications, 2004.

Mills, J. P. *The Lotha Nagas*. London: Macmillan & Co., 1922.

Mohanty, P. K. *Encyclopedia of Scheduled Tribes in India* (5 Volumes). New Delhi: Gyan Publishing House, 2006.

Mullik, B. N. *My Years with Nehru: The Chinese Betrayal*. New Delhi: Allied Publishers, 1971.

Muthukumaraswamy, M. D. *Folklore as Discourse*. Chennai: National Folklore Support Centre, 2006.

Nath, D. *History of the Koch Kingdom, c. 1515–1615*. New Delhi: Mittal Publications, 1989.

Nagaraju, N., and Byomakesh Tripathy. *Cultural Heritage of Arunachal Pradesh*. New Delhi: Indus Publishing Company, 2006.

Nanda, Neeru. *Tawang, The Land of Mon*. New Delhi: Vikas Publishing House, 1982.

Negi, Sharad Singh. *Himalayan Rivers, Lakes and Glaciers*. New Delhi: Indus Publishing Company, 1991.

Nongkynrih, Aurelius Kyrham. *Khasi Society of Meghalaya: A Sociological Understanding*. New Delhi: Indus Publishing Company, 2002.

Nyori, Tai. *History and Culture of the Adis*. New Delhi: Omsons Publications, 1993.

Palit, D. K. *Sentinels of the North-East: The Assam Rifles*. New Delhi: Palit & Palit, 1984.

Palit, D. K. *War in High Himalaya: The Indian Army in Crisis, 1962*. London: C Hurst & Co. Publishers, 1991.

Pandey, Deepak. *History of Arunachal Pradesh: Earliest Times to 1972 AD*. Pasighat: Bani Mandir Publication, 1997.

Parratt, John. *Wounded Land: Politics & Identity in Modern Manipur*. New Delhi: Mittal Publications, 2005.

Parratt, Saroj Nalini Arambam. *The Court Chronicle of the Kings of Manipur: The Cheitharol Kumpapa*. London: Routledge, 2005.

Pathak, Guptajit, and Raju Gogoi. *Cultural Fiesta in the "Island of Peace" Arunachal Pradesh*. New Delhi: Mittal Publications, 2008.

Pillai, Sushil Kumar. *Asam Vikram, Unique Valour: History of the Assam Regiment 1947-2002*. New Delhi: Macmillan, 2004.

Prakash, Ved. *Encyclopaedia of North-East India*. New Delhi: Atlantic Publishers & Distributers, 2007.

Puthenpurakal, Joseph. *Impact of Christianity on North East India*. Shillong: Vendrame Institute Publications, 1996.

Rajkumar, Falguni. *Rainbow People: Reinventing Northeast India*. New Delhi: Manas Publications, 2011.

Rikam, Nabam Tadar. *Emerging Religious Identities of Arunachal Pradesh: A Study of Nyishi Tribe*. New Delhi: Mittal Publications, 2005.

Roy, Ratna. *The Raj and the Princely State of Cooch Behar: A Study of Anglo-Cooch Behar Relations*. New Delhi: Dipali Publishers, 2004.

Roy, Sachin. *Aspects of Padam Minyong Culture*. Shillong: North East Frontier Agency, 1960.

Rustomji, Nari. *Enchanted Frontiers: Sikkim, Bhutan and India's Northeastern Borderlands*. New Delhi: Oxford University Press, 1971.

Saikia, Yasmin. *Fragmented Memories: Struggling to be Tai-Ahom in India*. Durham, NC: Duke University Press, 2004.

Saraswathi, Swami Sri Ramanananda. *Tripura Rahasya: The Secret of the Supreme Goddess*. Bloomington, IN: World Wisdom Inc., 2002.

Sasananda, S. *History of Buddhism in Assam, c. 300 BC–1200 AD*. New Delhi: Bahri Publications, 1986.

Sharma, N., and S. P. Shukla. *Geography and Development of Hill Areas: A Case Study of Arunachal Pradesh*, New Delhi: Mittal Publications, 1992.

Sharma, P. C. *Traditional Customs and Rituals of Northeast India*, Chennai: Vivekananda Kendra Prakashan Trust, 2004.

Sharma, Suresh Kumar, and Usha Sharma. "Assam: 1936 to 1957". From *Documents on North-East India: An Exhaustive Survey*, vol. no. 4. New Delhi: Mittal Publications, 2006.

Sharma, Suresh Kumar, and Usha Sharma. "Assam: 1958 to Modern Times". From *Documents on North-East India: An Exhaustive Survey*, vol. no. 5. New Delhi: Mittal Publications, 2006.

Sharma, Suresh Kumar, and Usha Sharma. "Meghalaya". From *Documents on North-East India: An Exhaustive Survey*, vol. no. 7. New Delhi: Mittal Publications, 2006.

Sharma, Suresh Kumar, and Usha Sharma. "Sikkim". From *Documents on North-East India: An Exhaustive Survey*, vol. no. 10. New Delhi: Mittal Publications, 2005.

Showren, Tana. *The Nyishi of Arunachal Pradesh: An Ethnohistorical Study*. New Delhi: Regency Publications, 2009.

Singh, Chandrika. *North-East India: Politics and Insurgency*. New Delhi: Manas Publications, 2007.

Singh, Kumar Suresh, S. H. M. Rizvi, and M. Horam. *People of India: Assam*. New Delhi: Anthropological Survey of India, Ministry of Culture, 2003.

Singh, Kumar Suresh, Arabinda Basu, and Shibani Roy. *People of India: Meghalaya*. New Delhi: Anthropological Survey of India, Ministry of Culture, 1994.

Singh, Kumar Suresh. *People of India: Sikkim*, New Delhi: Anthropological Survey of India, Ministry of Culture, 1993.

Singh, Kumar Suresh, Sekhara Bandyopadhyaya, Tilak Bagchi, and R. K. Bhattacharya. *People of India: West Bengal*. New Delhi: Anthropological Survey of India, Ministry of Culture, 2003.

Singh, Thingnam Kishan. *Look East Policy and India's North East: Polemics and Perspectives*. Manipur: Centre for Alternative Discourse, 2009.

Singh, Amar Kaur Jasbir. *Himalayan Triangle: Historical Survey of British India's Relations with Tibet, Sikkim and Bhutan, 1765–1950*. London: British Library, 1988.

Singh, Kumar Suresh. *People of India: Arunachal Pradesh*. New Delhi: Anthropological Survey of India, 1992.

Tada, Tage, and B. J. Das. *A Descriptive Account of the Sculptures of Malinithan*. Itanagar: Government of Arunachal Pradesh, 2003.

Tayeng, Obang. *Folktales of the Adis*. New Delhi: Mittal Publications, 2007.

Tayeng, Obang. *Mishmi Folk Tales of Lohit Valley*. New Delhi: Mittal Publications, 2007.

Vas, E. A. *The Dragon Kingdom: Journeys Through Bhutan*, New Delhi: Lancer Publications, 1984.

Vergese, C. G., and R. L. Thanzawna. *History of the Mizos*, New Delhi: Vikas Publications, 1997.

Verma, Ashok Kalyan. *Rivers of Silence: Disaster on River Nam Ka Chu, 1962*. New Delhi: Lancer Publications, 1998.

Verma, Shiv Kunal, and Dipti Bhalla. *Assam Rifles: 1835–2010*, Gurgaon: KaleidoIndia, 2010.

Verma, Shiv Kunal. *1962: The War That Wasn't*. New Delhi: Aleph, 2016.

Index